MILLENNIAL ECONOMICS

Praise for *Millennial Economics*

The elegant writing and incisive explanations found in this volume conquer the complexity of the topic and its mixture of rhapsodic prose and an almost eerie moral clarity project with buoyancy and hope. The majority of laws in the Five Books of Moses concern money, and this important volume, while reflecting the spontaneous surgings of the human spirit, helps us understand why.

—Rabbi Daniel Lapin,
American Alliance of Jews and Christians

Other books by Victor Shane

Book of Life
God, Cosmos, and Man: A New Understanding of Human Nature

In God We Trust
Understanding the Culture War in a Scientific Age: The Pitched Battle for the Soul of America

DDDB: Drag Device Data Base
Using Parachutes, Sea Anchors, and Drogues to Cope with Heavy Weather: Over 120 Documented Case Histories

MILLENNIAL ECONOMICS

An American Declaration of Independence
from Central Banking—A Global Transition
to Debt-Free National Economies

Victor Shane

Foreword by Rabbi Daniel Lapin

WestBow
PRESS
A DIVISION OF THOMAS NELSON

WestBow Press books may be ordered through booksellers or by contacting:

WestBow Press
A Division of Thomas Nelson
1663 Liberty Drive
Bloomington, IN 47403
www.westbowpress.com
1-(866) 928-1240

Unless otherwise indicated, Scripture quotations are from the King James Version of the Bible. Revised Standard Version of the Bible, copyright 1952, by the Division of Christian Education of the National Council of Churches of Christ in the United States.

ISBN: 978-1-4497-9052-3 (sc)
ISBN: 978-1-4497-9055-4 (hc)
ISBN: 978-1-4497-9051-6 (e)

Library of Congress Control Number: 2013906052

Printed in the United States of America.

WestBow Press rev. date: 06/10/2013

For Michael, Beverly, Jerry, Sam, Gary, Robert, Conrad, Brad, Aaron, Daniel, Steve, Jeff, Cameron, Mike, Cornelius, Jason, Rod, Jack, Rich, Peter, David, Inga-Lill, Troy, Drew, Nate, Scott, Ted, Doug, Jeremy, Trevor, John, Isaac, Keith, Rob, Shayne, Bailey, Eileen, Karen, Carol, Sadie, Nathan, Kristen, Dave, Nanci, Ellen, Lars, Emily, Lydia, and Lindy Grace.

Our national debt is our biggest national security threat.
—Admiral Mike Mullen,
Chairman of the Joint Chiefs of Staff,
June 24, 2010

Contents

Acknowledgments

I will not attempt to list all the individuals whose advice and suggestions have helped launch this publication. I would be remiss, however, if I did not mention some of them.

I'd like to thank Rabbi Daniel Lapin of the American Alliance for Jews and Christians for his enormous contributions to my own understanding of the biblical underpinnings of the uniquely American concepts of free enterprise and wealth creation; my editor, Paul Conant, for his meticulous attention to detail—not to mention invaluable advice and many helpful criticisms; and lawyer, editor, friend, and learned sage Channing Bates, for adding a depth of philosophical, historical, political, and economic savvy to my own understanding of the subjects covered in this book.

I would especially like to extend my heartfelt gratitude to my Calvary Chapel Marketplace Ministry brethren: Michael, Mike, Jerry, Sam, Conrad, Brad, Aaron, Daniel, Dan, Steve, Jeff, Cameron, Jack, Cornelius, Jason, Rich, and others at Calvary Chapel for their continual prayers and supplications asking heaven to provide me with clarity of thought and critical insights, without which I would not have tackled the monumental problem of global debt, a problem that is now competing against the labor of man and seeking to deprive him of the dignity of his origins in God.

Foreword

Have you noticed that people say things like, "Open communication is the lifeblood of this organization," or "A reliable fuel supply is the lifeblood of this airline"? But they seldom say, "New members are the gallbladder of this club," or "Busy bureaucrats are the big toe of government." What is so special about blood?

Like Superman swooping in to the rescue, here comes ancient Jewish wisdom with the answer. In the Lord's language, Hebrew, when one word is used for two apparently separate concepts, those two ideas are really very connected to one another. The Hebrew word for blood DAMIM is identical to one of the words used throughout the ancient writings of Jewish wisdom to mean money.

Blood = DAMIM = Money

What are the similarities between blood and money? Both money and blood are most useful in quantity. The singular of both words is seldom used. "I need some blood" but never "I need a blood." "Can you lend me a money?" No, I don't think so. Blood and money comprise countless individual elements, each one identifiable, but needing to be aggregated with many others to be useful. Blood is made up of countless units called red and white cells, and money is made up of countless units such as pennies or dollars.

Both blood and money are relatively fungible (freely exchangeable or replaceable). When you borrow my car, I want that car, not a similar one, returned. On the other hand, when you pay me back the ten dollars I loaned you on Friday, I really don't care that it is not exactly the same ten-dollar bill I gave you. In fact, you can even write me a check. Organs like a heart or liver often get rejected when transferred from one person to another, which makes transplants very challenging. Blood, however, can be moved from person to person with comparative ease, just like money.

Both blood and money need to circulate in order to be effective. Bags of blood can contribute to human health; but merely sitting on the shelf in the blood bank, they aren't doing their job. It is just the same for bags of money. They are not doing anyone any good merely sitting on the shelf in the money bank. That is why when people fearfully hoard their dollars rather than spending or investing them, our economy totters.

Finally, both blood and money carry nourishment to the farthest reaches of the organism, whether a country or a body. If blood is cut off from an extremity of the body, like a toe, the toe will die. When a customer in Maine buys goods from a seller in the remote foothills of the Rockies, the entire country thrives.

The medium of exchange necessary for that transaction is money. When a craftsman in Africa sells a bracelet to a teacher in England, money has made that craftsman healthier, just like a blood transfusion would.

By using the identical word for blood and money, ancient Jewish wisdom teaches that our money is indeed our financial lifeblood and must be treated every bit as seriously as our real blood. For instance, a hemorrhage of either entity must be stopped and treated immediately. Tainted blood and tainted money both have the power to destroy life. Unfortunately, many of us fail to take financial first aid as seriously as we do medical first aid.

This powerful money-blood principle of viewing your money as almost as important as your blood is one of the keys to why, throughout history, Jews have been disproportionately good with money. Fortunately, this key is now available to all, regardless of religious heritage.

—Rabbi Daniel Lapin
American Alliance of Jews and Christians
www.RabbiDanielLapin.com

Author's Introduction

Democracy, the antidote to tyranny, and in many ways one of the greatest gifts of God to mankind, involves a process of emancipation whereby something that was once available or accessible to a privileged few becomes available and accessible to many. Looking at the grand picture of history, one might say, for example, that the Pauline Gospel democratized the kingdom of God, or that the Reformation democratized Christianity, or that America's Founding Fathers democratized government.

Alternatively, one might say the printing press democratized knowledge; schools democratized education; universities democratized science; free enterprise democratized wealth creation; the telephone democratized communication; the automobile democratized transportation; the Internet democratized information; and so on and so forth.

Indeed, looking at the big picture of history we see every providence, every blessing, every gift of God, every useful convenience, conveyance, and contraption being made available to many, in the fullness of time. Through it all, however, one thing has resisted all efforts at democratization: the apparatus of money creation, specifically, the seventeenth-century scaffolding of central banking that is now competing against the labor of man and seeking to deprive him of the dignity of his origins in God.

For too long the issues of money creation, introduction, and manipulation have been left ill-defined and unresolved, to this day regarded as occult sciences hidden behind a cloud of mystery and technical jargon accessible only by a privileged few. To compound matters, the last two decades have produced a financial elite who speak a language of their own, live in isolated silos, and seem to possess arcane powers that they can use to amass fortunes on the backs of public ruin.

How did this happen? No doubt part of the reason has had to do with unawareness and a general lack of wisdom on the part of "We the People." Just mention collateralized debt obligations (CDOs), mortgaged backed securities (MBSs), or credit-default swaps (CDSs), and otherwise intelligent Americans will freeze like deer in headlights and then walk away muttering, "This stuff is over my head!"

There is a need for a *cultural translator* to come along and deconstruct the complicated-sounding jargon to the point where "We the People" can understand what is going on and what we must do to avoid the financial catastrophes that are now just around the corner.

Millennial Economics was written to serve as a cultural translator. The first chapter takes the form of a Wall Street morality play staged onboard a luxurious corporate jet bound for Bermuda. Onboard are two men, white-haired Saul Pearlzandt and his son, Wall Street billionaire John Pearlzandt. Saul is financially naïve but curious and concerned. He wants to know how his son managed to make so many billions of dollars overnight. As the two confront each other at an altitude of twenty thousand feet, Saul demands that his son explain complicated financial matters to him in plain English.

At first John is evasive and keeps trying to change the subject. But Saul is relentless. The sparring between father and son is heated and penetrating, but in the end the reader comes away with a holistic understanding of CDOs, MBSs, and CDSs.

As the Wall Street morality play ends in chapter 1, subsequent chapters of *Millennial Economics* begin to deconstruct the puzzles of money creation, central banking, Federal Reserve theory, inflation, gold standard, national debt, recession, depression, etc., with a view toward informing, educating, and empowering "We the People." All this is a prelude to achieving the auspicious goal of removing the millstone of impossible debt from the back of nations and replacing the crumbling seventeenth-century scaffolding of central banking with a just, fair, and equitable system of trade and commerce throughout the whole world.

Chapter 1

The Great Coffin Trade:
The Ribald Wager against the American Dream

My defense is that I operate within the rules. If there is a breakdown in the rules, that is not my fault as a lawful participant but the fault of those who set the rules.—George Soros, *Soros on Soros: Staying Ahead of the Curve*

G aunt and white-haired Saul Pearlzandt's secret mission on the trip was to try to get his son, now-famous Wall Street billionaire John Pearlzandt, to explain in layman's terms how he had managed to make so much money in so short a time. A retired mathematics teacher with a penchant for classical music, Saul was an orthodox Jew with deep religious convictions and a genealogy going all the way back to the wise king Solomon. He was, on the one hand, proud of his son's newfound fame, fortune, and apparent ability to bring Wall Street giants to their knees, but on the other hand diffident about the ethics and morality of the whole business. Something just didn't seem kosher about the affair.

Saul hoped what his son had recently achieved had not only been legitimate, moral, aboveboard, and honest but in conformity with the Jewish ideal of *Tzedakah*.[1] To Saul Pearlzandt, making money was a lofty,

---

[1] *Tzedakah* is a profoundly Jewish concept rooted in the Hebrew *tzedek* words found in the Torah (Pentateuch), signifying justice, righteousness, uprightness, virtue, morality, rectitude, fairness, honesty, and integrity. Two prominent examples would be the powerful imperative found in Deuteronomy 16:20: *Tzedek, tzedek tirdof* ("Justice, justice you shall pursue"), and the equally potent directive alluded to in Habakkuk 2:4 (later referred to by St. Paul in Romans 1:17 and later still used by Luther to lay the foundation of the Reformation): *V'tzaddik be'emunato yich'yeh* ("the righteous shall live by his faith").

1

noble, and uniquely *American* profession, involving honesty, integrity, good
reputation, stick-to-itiveness, human cooperation, and many years of hard
work, resulting in the personal wealth that opened the door to giving,
philanthropy, charity, responsibility, generosity, goodwill, kindness, and
all the other good and noble things associated with *tzedakah*. But this?
This other thing that his son had managed to pull off overnight—what
was that all about?

To make matters worse, he had heard rumors that some people were
pointing fingers at his son, accusing John of being one of the masterminds
behind the recent subprime mortgage meltdown. Saul could only hope
the accusations were groundless, but John had been evasive up to now,
and try as he might, Saul couldn't get any straight answers out of him. He
needed to sit down with his son, discuss the whole thing, and clear the air
and his conscience, not to mention the family name. So this was it—his
opportunity to do exactly that.

As the gleaming white Pearlzandt & Co. Gulfstream jet leveled off
at twenty thousand feet, a pleasant bell was heard, the seatbelt light
went off, and father and son found themselves alone and face-to-face,
reclining in plush leather armchairs in the executive jet's luxurious
interior. Grinning like a little boy, John reached into a side panel,
produced something looking like an iPad, and began acquainting his
father with all the hi-tech cabin fixtures that he could manipulate via
remote control. As he did so, the scent of his expensive cologne mingled
with the smell of the new leather upholstery of the aircraft interior,
adding an air of intrigue and opulence to the get-together Saul felt
somewhat uncomfortable with. The muffled sound of the outside air
rushing by at five hundred miles per hour made the ambiance all the
more strange and extravagant.

At this rate they would be in Bermuda in a few hours, where John had
promised to wine and dine his father on the occasion of Saul's seventy-
seventh birthday a few days away. Just then the rear galley door opened
and a smart-looking stewardess in a chic uniform walked in to offer the
CEO and his white-haired father sparkling libation.

John, wearing designer sporting attire and $300 tennis shoes, smiled
proudly at his father. "A little champagne, Papa?" As the stewardess presented
the fancy bottle to Saul, John pointed to the label: "Dom *Pérignon* ... Dom

Pérignon White Gold Jeroboam, one of the most expensive champagnes in the world!"

Saul, in wrinkled suit and tie, shrugged without smiling. "Why, thank you, boy, don't mind if I do." There was no enthusiasm in his voice.

The stewardess poured the bubbly into elegant champagne glasses, smiled gracefully, placed the bottle in the ice-filled decanter, and retreated from the cabin. Saul thanked her politely and asked that they be not disturbed.

John took a sip of the expensive champagne and, still grinning like a little boy, continued toying with the remote control, making the window blinds go up and down, the cabin lights go dim and bright, flat-panel screens slide in and out of their stylish housings. The spectacle reminded Saul of John's fifth birthday when he had given him his first bicycle, that happy occasion in which he had spent the whole day running alongside his son's precarious perch on the two-wheeler, steadying him, encouraging him, picking him up when he fell, dusting him off, and putting him back on the saddle until finally, with scraped knees and bruised elbows, John could pedal the bicycle back and forth all by himself, ringing the bell and shouting, "Look, Papa! Look!"

John brought the remote control close so his father could see it and tapped the little screen to roll out the hi-tech speakers elegantly camouflaged within the cabin of the Gulfstream jet. "Listen to this, Papa!" There was excitement in his voice as he tapped the screen again and the speakers came to life in magnificent surround sound with the opening passages of Ernest Bloch's "Sacred Service" from the *Avodath Hakodesh*, the choral symphony the Pearlzandt family had known Grandpa Saul to listen to with tears in his eyes. John smiled proudly as he increased the volume, and the music and choral voices began to envelop them with their spiritual dimensions.

Saul, however, seemed unmoved. Presently he had other things on his mind. He wanted to seize the initiative and start the conversation going in the right direction before his son could shanghai it elsewhere. He asked John to turn off the music and put down the remote control, which John did. He then looked his son squarely in the eyes and began to speak slowly, carefully, and deliberately.

"So, John ... six months ago, shortly after Rosh Hashanah, we were going to have some father-and-son quality time together ... you were going to explain Wall Street to me and how you made so many billions of dollars overnight. But we never got around to it, did we?"

John sensed what was coming and couldn't help tensing up a bit. He knew his father to be a highly principled, disciplined, ethical, and honorable man, and his gut feeling told him he was in for the grilling of his life. This was the moment of truth, and short of donning a parachute and bailing out of the jet, there was no escaping the ordeal to come.

He cleared his throat, but his reply was still hoarse and sounded like a feeble excuse. "Well, yes, Papa, we were going to get together … but, you know how it goes … Wall Street never sleeps … a few things came up … and then there was that subpoena from the House of Representatives' Committee on Oversight, which I couldn't very well ignore … could I?"

Saul, sharp as a razor at seventy-six, about to turn seventy-seven, could already see his son attempting evasion and subterfuge. He remembered chastising John when he was a little boy, and it seemed like the scenario was repeating itself, a déjà vu.

He brushed aside John's feeble excuses with a firm voice. "Ya, okay, boy, never mind all that! We're here now, just the two of us, about to have quality time and clear up a few things that have been bothering me recently." Bothering him? The recent subprime mortgage meltdown had sent global economies reeling and caused millions of families to lose their homes and livelihoods! The idea that his son might have had *something* to do with the sordid business had been giving Saul no end of sleepless nights!

John smiled compassionately at the virtuous father he loved and respected, but then for some unknown reason he began laughing. It was a nervous laugh, with guilt written all over it, and they both knew it.

Hearing John laugh like that, Saul put down his champagne glass and began to stare at him in stony silence. This was the icy stare of displeasure John had been exposed to as a little boy and dreaded even now. He had no defense against it. The look in his father's eyes was enough to make him want to repent of his sins and immoral lusts.

He stopped laughing, cleared his voice again, and sat up straight. "Okay, Papa, okay, you win! Quality time is here, and you can start the interrogation—where do you want to begin? What do you want to know?"

Saul raised the champagne glass to his lips, took a casual sip, looked about, and fired off the first of his well-rehearsed questions, trying not sound like a judge at an inquisition. "For starters, boy, I want to know all about *short trades* and *put options* ... explain them to me!"

John was a little surprised by the question and was momentarily overcome by his father's innocence and naiveté when it came to the inner workings of Wall Street. He laughed nervously again and then leaned toward his father, looked around mischievously as though trying to make sure no one else was listening, smiled, and whispered the words in Saul's ear as though divulging a great secret: "*Short trades* and *put options*, Papa, involve taking positions in the market!"

"Huh? What?" Saul couldn't help blurting out his reaction. "Positions? What's that? What does that mean, taking positions?"

John leaned back pensively. "It means ... well, it means you are taking a position in the market in which you are ... hmmm, how should I put it ... you are *selling it without owning it and agree to return it at the end of a specified time period.*"

Saul paused and leaned back for a few moments, trying to dissect the words he had just heard. He seemed bewildered. "I don't get it!" he said. "What do you mean 'selling it'? Selling what? How can you sell something you don't own and then return it after you've sold it?"

John retreated into his armchair, took a generous sip of Dom *Pérignon*, and tried to savor the brief moment of triumph in which he had his father at a disadvantage. He nonchalantly waved his hand about his head. "There's nothing to it, Papa! Traders do it all the time. All you need is a willing seller, a willing buyer, a broker, and money to back up the trade. There's no shortage of buyers, sellers, or brokers on Wall Street, and you can always find some banker to lend you the money for the trade."

Try as he might, Saul couldn't banish the look of stupid bewilderment from his wrinkled and wiry face. He too waved his hand in the air, shook his head, and was about to say something but then decided to take a sip of champagne to calm his nerves. "I still don't get it," he said, quietly. "Why don't I get it? I think I'm a fairly intelligent person ... I used to teach mathematics at Purdue. I mean I'm not a *schlemiel*, am I? So why don't I get it, boy?"

John knew *schlemiel* to be a Yiddish word describing a stupid person and was quick to scold his father for applying it to himself. "Don't say that, Papa! As far as I'm concerned you're one of the wisest men in the universe!"

"Well, I still don't get it," was his reply. "I mean, how does the whole thing work? Who authorizes it? Who's in charge? Who makes the rules? Who's running the show?"

"The syndicate."

"The syndicate? What syndicate?"

"The syndicate, Papa."

Saul shook his head in puzzlement. But then he realized they were starting to get off topic, exactly what he wanted to avoid. "Ya, okay, John, syndicate, shmyndicate … whatever! But you still haven't explained *short trades* and *put options* to me."

John looked about pensively and then drew nearer to his father. "Hmmm, let me see … how can I make it easier for you to understand? Try to think of it in this way: you borrow something for a fee and can do whatever you want with it for a set period before you have to return it."

"Borrow what? From whom?"

"Let's say borrow stock, from a willing stock owner."

"And why on earth would a stock owner let me borrow his stock and do whatever I want with it?"

"Because, Papa, you will be paying him cold hard cash for the rental."

Saul withdrew, looking more puzzled than ever. "Oy vey, John! I still don't get it! Give me an example, I mean an example that even a *schlemiel* can understand … ya?"

John's face registered momentary suspicion in the realization that his white-haired father was now donning his infamous Yiddish disguise. In Yiddish disguise, "yes" became *ya*, "woe!" became *Oy vey!*, and "good grief!" became *oy gevalt!* In Yiddish disguise, *maven* was a cynical way of referring to an "expert," a *schlemiel* was a clumsy idiot, *spiel* described a long, involved sales pitch, *mazel tov* was a sarcastic way of saying "good luck with that!," and *feh!* was the term used to register utter disgust.

Saul's Yiddish disguise was a crafty, self-negating, self-denigrating ruse that he was known to employ when he wanted to drag something out of family members. It was a clever strategy calculated to make family member feel sorry for Papa, which always resulted in Papa getting what he wanted.

John couldn't help rolling his eyes in frustration. "You want an example?"

"Yes, John. Your father wants an example!"

John thought for a moment, and then a light bulb seemed to go on in his head and his face lit up. "Okay, Papa, I think there's a good example in one of the latest James Bond movies ... it was called, uh, *Casino Royale* ... yes, *Casino Royale*. Did you see it?"

Saul thought for a moment. "Ya ... I seem to remember. Bobi dragged me and the grandkids to the local theatre to see James Bond ... handsome secret agent, driving fast cars, shooting people, and playing poker ... but I don't remember anything about *short trades* or *put options* in it."

John sat up and feigned exaggerated surprise. "Papa? You fell asleep in the movie again?" As the large Pearlzandt family loved to go to movies together, and as Grandpa Saul had a reputation for falling asleep and snoring loudly in the movie, John couldn't help getting off the slight, hoping it would defuse some of the tension building between them.

"Never mind the wisecracks!" came the harsh reply.

John continued. "Well, Papa, if you didn't fall asleep in that James Bond movie, then you may remember the part about the villain *shorting* the stock of an airline called ... I think it was called Skyfleet or something like that ... do you remember that part?"

"Ya? And?"

"Well, the villain wanted to make a lot of money *betting against* Skyfleet stock, so he borrowed a million shares of Skyfleet and—"

"He *borrowed* a million shares of Skyfleet stock?"

"Yes, borrowed, rented ... you can think of it in those terms ... it makes it easier for you to get the basic picture."

"Okay, so he rented a million shares of Skyfleet?"

"Yes. Then, as it were, he went to the stock market, sold those million shares at the going price, and put the cash in his pocket. Think of it like that."

"He rented and sold a million shares of Skyfleet belonging to someone else and put the cash in his pocket?"

"Yes, but knowing that, *regardless of the future price*, he would have to return a million shares of Skyfleet to the stock owner before the trade expired."

Saul was having a hard time coming to terms with what he was hearing but wanted to get on with it nevertheless. "Ya, okay, John, so what did the villain do next?"

"He hired a terrorist to go and blow up Skyfleet's prototype passenger jetliner as it was being unveiled at the Miami airport."

"And what would that have accomplished?"

"With the prototype blown up, Skyfleet's stock would have tumbled in value and the villain could have used the cash in his pocket to buy back a million shares of Skyfleet at pennies on the dollar ..."

"In which case ...?"

"In which case he could have returned a million shares of Skyfleet to the stock owner before the trade expired and pocketed the difference in millions of dollars. Except, of course, James Bond foiled the terrorist's plot, and the villain ended up having to buy back the stock at a much higher price, losing his shirt in the process ... but I digress."

Saul thought he was beginning to see a basic outline of things. "Ya, okay, boy, let me get this straight. You rent stock from a willing stock owner and pay him a fee for the rental, which makes him happy, ya? You go to the stock market and sell the stock when the price is higher, ya? Later you go back to the stock market and buy it back when the price is lower, ya? Then you return the stock to its owner before the trade expires and pocket the difference, ya? And that's known as a short trade?"

John gave a weak nod. "Well, more or less. Basically you are *betting against* a stock—wagering that its value will go down instead of up. If you are *shorting* a stock, or a bond, or a currency, or a security, or a treasury, or whatever, you are betting that its value will go down in time so that you can buy it back at the bottom of the market and pocket the difference before the trade expires ..."

"Sounds very complicated!"

"Not really, Papa. These trades are actually quite transparent and seamless."

"What does that mean, 'transparent and seamless'?"

"It just means your broker handles everything for you. You don't have to know the stock owner. You don't have to go to the stock market to sell the rented stock when its value is higher, and then go back to the stock market again to buy it back when its value is lower. You pay your broker a fee to do all of this for you automatically, and he takes care of the whole thing behind the scenes, just like in the James Bond movie."

Saul couldn't help shaking his head in amazement. "Oy vey, John! That was just a Hollywood movie."

"Yes, Papa, but short trades are real enough. You remember 9/11, when terrorists flew those passenger jets into the Twin Towers of the World Trade Center in New York? Afterward, when the authorities investigated everything, it turned out someone had made a lot of money *shorting* airline stocks ..."

"Meaning what?"

"Meaning what I just explained to you."

"Explain it to me again, boy."

"Meaning just before 9/11, someone, somewhere in the world, may have known what was about to happen and taken up massive short positions on airline stocks. After 9/11, when airline stocks hit rock bottom, whoever it was walked away with millions of dollars."

Upon hearing this, the look on Saul's face changed from one of bewildered curiosity to one of utter disgust. The next words to emerge from his vocal chords came as whispers and sounded downright morbid: "Feh! Coffin trade."

"Coffin trade, Papa?"

"Coffin trade. What else do you want me to call it?"

John was speechless. For a moment he sat there with his mouth agape, seeing his father's innocent outlook at loggerheads with the dog-eat-dog narrative of the financial world.

Saul sat silently for a few moments, his head bowed in disgust, wondering what manner of depravity in human nature might have the capacity to engineer a tragedy like 9/11 and the savvy to make millions of dollars *shorting* airline stocks in the process. But he didn't want to get bogged down or sidetracked with 9/11. Time was short, and he had bigger questions that needed answers. "That brings me to my next question, boy—what is a *put option*?"

John took another generous sip from his champagne glass before answering. "A put option, Papa, is more or less the same as a short trade ...

except you don't need as much security on deposit in your brokerage account."

"You don't have to put up security?"

"No. You can just instruct your broker to go and get you some *put option contracts* ..."

"Put option contracts? Give me an example of one."

"Well, for example, you could tell your broker to go and buy you some 'Skyfleet September $100 put options.'"

"Skyfleet September $100 put options?"

"Yes, Skyfleet September $100 put options ... as an example."

"And what would this do?"

"This would lock in the stock price for you ..."

"What does that mean, 'Lock in the stock price'?"

"It means regardless of changing market prices, your put option would give you the right, but not the obligation, to sell Skyfleet stock for $100 a share until the September options expiration date—third Friday in September."

"And I could use this put option to bet against Skyfleet stock with no money down, eh? That's a nice game!"

"Yes, well ... you would have to pay a fee to buy the put option contract in the first place."

"I have to pay to play? Oh, good, that makes me feel better about the whole thing. Ya, okay, John, go on, go on."

"Well, Papa, if the Skyfleet stock price were to fall below $100, say to $80, you could then exercise your *option* to sell Skyfleet stock for $100 a share and then buy it back at $80 for a nice $20 profit, raking in $20 million from one million shares. Just imagine how much money you could rake in if the stock price were to fall to ten dollars a share!"

John was smiling politely at his father, but there was condescension in his voice. He sounded like a teacher having a hard time explaining something routine and simple to an obstinate and inattentive student. "Are you getting the basic picture, Papa? If the stock value goes down before the *put* expires, you can make money. If the price stays the same or goes up, you can just let your *option* expire as worthless, and the only money you lose is what you paid your broker in fees."

"Hmm ... how do I get into this racket?" Saul asked sarcastically.

"Well, it's not difficult ... and you wouldn't have to do much yourself. Your broker could take care of everything for you. In this case, for example, he could simply sell your put contract on an options exchange and send you a big fat check." John continued, trying to force a cheerful face, but there was growing impatience in his voice. He would have liked to change the subject and bring closure to Saul's probing questions, but he could tell his father was determined to pursue the interrogation to conclusion regardless of what it might do to their relationship.

Saul continued. "Ya, okay, John, I see! A put option is another *bet-to-fail* contract, ya? Another coffin trade, but with a different varnish ... and now you can bury Skyfleet in it with no money down." The sarcasm was palpable in Saul's voice.

"Yes, well, I suppose you could call it a bet-to-fail contract, Papa, but I wouldn't go so far as to call it a coffin trade ... and frankly, I don't know what you mean by 'coffin trade' ..."

"I mean cashing in on someone else's demise and profiting from someone else's ruin. That's what I mean!"

John had to smile even more politely before responding. "Well, that sort of thing may be James Bond fiction, but in the real world there are only willing sellers and willing buyers. And, 9/11 notwithstanding, those who take *short positions* in the market don't go around hiring terrorists to do evil things to bring down the stock prices they're betting against."

Saul took a deep breath and exhaled with a great sigh of displeasure, disillusionment, and disappointment. "I don't get it, John. Maybe I'm too old-fashioned to understand these coffin trades and bet-to-fail shenanigans. Why would anyone want to use short trades and put options to invest in failure, misery, ruin, and demise? Why would they not want to invest in success instead? Isn't that the American way? Isn't that what the traditional stock market was supposed to be all about?" He shook his head in sadness. "I don't know ... this whole thing doesn't seem kosher to me!"

"It may not seem kosher to you, Papa, but, well, that's how it's set up ... and that's how it works. If you're careful, if you do your homework, if you know what you're doing, if you know the trends and the markets, and if know what's going on in the business world, you can use short trades and put options to make a lot of money overnight … a lot faster than you would from the traditional way of investing in stocks and sometimes waiting for years to rake in dividends."

Saul continued shaking his head. "I don't know, John. It still doesn't seem right. And who was it who came up with these bet-to-fail shenanigans? Who was it who made these coffin trades possible in the first place? Whose idea was it? Who's running the show?"

"The syndicate!"

"Again with the syndicate?"

"Yes, the syndicate."

"Who is this syndicate?"

"It's everybody, Papa!"

Saul had a mind to pursue this notion of "the syndicate" further but again steadied himself, remembering that time was short, they would be landing in Bermuda soon, and now was not the time to go chasing after red herrings.

John, already feeling the strain of the interrogation, had to force another polite smile, pour himself more Dom Pérignon, and try to maintain a cheerful face. "Next question, Papa?"

Saul was also beginning to feel the strain, but he had come prepared. He put on his reading glasses, reached into his pocket, and nonchalantly pulled out a piece of paper with a list on it.

John was quick to protest: "Good grief, Papa. I can't believe this! You brought a list? And on our vacation to Bermuda?"

Saul ignored his son's quip and rattled off his next question. "A *CDO*. What is it? Explain a CDO to me!"

John leaned over and tried to get a glimpse of the other things his father had scribbled on the piece of paper, but Saul covered it with his hand. "By CDO I presume you're referring to *collateralized debt obligations*?"

"Ya … that!"

John leaned back, looked at the ceiling, and took his time answering. "Well, a CDO is a new type of financial instrument. But if you really want to understand what it is, first you have to understand two other principles."

"Which are?"

"The reality principle, and the *securitization*[2] principle."

"Sounds complicated, but I'm all ears, boy! Tell your father the whole story. What's the reality principle all about?"

"It's all about debt. Private debt, public debt, debt with no end in sight. The grim and eternal reality of debt," John said, trying to sound chipper. Then, as though moved by some unknown impulse, he stood up, waved his arms about, and began singing with an operatic voice like that of a nervous cantor: "Debt in the morning, debt in the evening, debt at suppertime ..."

"Never mind the song and dance, boy," was the harsh rebuke. "Music was never one of your strong points. Sit down and explain CDOs to your father—*sit down*!"

John obediently sat. "Well, you see, everywhere in the world you have the same fundamental reality: debt."

"Ya ... so?"

"Think, Papa. What's so real about debt?"

"I don't know. What's so real about debt?"

"Well, it's not abstract numbers on bank ledgers, is it?"

"No? Then what is it?"

"It's monthly payments! Debt-related *cash flow*! All over the world, millions of people are continually in the *process* of making payments on what they owe. They are in the *process* of making monthly loan payments, monthly mortgage payments, monthly car payments, monthly credit card payments. Every month, billions and billions of dollars are in the *process* of flowing into debt pools in the form of payments."

"What debt pools? Try to be more clear, boy."

"Think of it as a big box. As people, businesses, institutions,

---

[2] In the deregulated environment (in which banking and Wall Street are allowed to more or less merge), *securitization* typically refers to a process of grouping/pooling tangible assets such as homes, buildings, and properties, and through paper manipulation(s) transforming them into "securities" that can be traded (or wagered against) by financial agents, investment bankers, and Wall Street speculators. An example would be the so-called *Mortgage-Backed Security* (MBS). More than anything else it was this process of so-called securitization that led to the declines in underwriting standards, whereby trillions of dollars of risky mortgages could suddenly be repackaged, repapered, and sold to investors around the world, setting the stage for the subprime mortgage meltdown and financial debacle of 2008.

municipalities, etc., make their monthly payments, the cash flows into a big box—"

"And that's a CDO?"

"No, a CDO is … well, now you have to understand the *debt securitization* principle."

"Debt securitization principle?"

"Yes. You see, a CDO is created when that payment process gets *securitized* into financial instruments that can be traded."

"I don't get it … what does that mean? How can you securitize a *process*?" Saul couldn't hide the frustration in his voice.

"Picture it like this: think of CDOs as a big box of incoming loan payments chopped up into different risk layers that can be traded as securities."

"A process can be chopped up into *risk layers* that can be traded as securities?"

"Yes, Papa."

"Says who?"

"The syndicate!"

"Again with the syndicate?"

"Yes, well, the fact is CDOs now exist and they *can* and *are* being traded as securities."

"You mean imaginary securities!"

"No … well … they're real enough. They're real enough because they are asset-backed—"

"Asset-backed, you say? Backed by what kind of assets? Risky subprime mortgages?"

Upon hearing the words "risky subprime mortgages," John tensed up a bit. "Yes, well, a mortgage is itself backed up by something real, isn't it? Like a house or an office building?" He didn't sound convincing.

Saul drew back. He squinted, as though sensing something phony about this whole "CDO" thing. He had previously Googled "CDO" and ran into explanations that in his considered opinion amounted to so much gobbledygook, so this was his opportunity of getting straight answers from the wizard of Wall Street himself—his own flesh and blood son!

"Okay. So, let me get this straight: CDOs—collateralized debt obligations—are like anticipated cash flows of incoming loan payments that someone has chopped up into risk layers that can be peddled as securities for speculators to wager with … ya?"

John didn't know what to say. "Well, I wouldn't put it quite that way—"

"And these different 'risk layers' … they're called *tranches*, ya?"

John's mouth opened wide with surprise and admiration. "Papa? You know about tranches?" He stood up and started clapping his hands.

"*Sit down!*" was the harsh rebuke. Saul would have none of his son's approbation. He turned his face away and seemed momentarily preoccupied. An elusive thought had filtered into his mind, and he wanted to grab it before it evaporated into thin air. "So, then, in reality, this whole CDO business is based on smoke and mirrors, ya? Based on an *assumption*, about a *process,* ya?"

"Yes, well, call it assumption, projection, whatever, but it's not smoke and mirrors. It's like what I said about the reality of debt. The whole world is in debt, and there will always be *some* money flowing into the big box."

Saul rocked back and forth in his armchair. As he did, the expression on his face changed from one of curious litigant to smiling skeptic. Suddenly he raised his voice and began pontificating: "There you have it, ladies and gentlemen! An assumption about a process becomes a pot of gold that can be chopped up into *casino chips* for speculators to gamble with! Welcome to the la-la-land of Wall Street!"

John had to object to this line of reasoning. "Well, yes, like I said, these 'casino chips,' as you call them, are in fact backed up with anticipated cash flows of monthly loan payments, mortgage payments, credit card payments—"

"Anticipated by whom? Moses and Elijah?"

"No, by the syndicate!"

"Again with the syndicate? Just who is this 'syndicate'?"

"It's everybody, Papa!"

Saul couldn't stop shaking his head. "I don't get it! In the fantasyland of Wall Street a process can be magically transformed, chopped up, leveraged, and inflated into billions of dollars' worth of imaginary securities? And what happens when the *process* slows down or stops? What happens when cash stops flowing into your make-believe box?"

"There'll always be *some* cash flowing into the big box … which can be broken up into asset-backed securities." John sounded like a schoolboy parroting something he had been made to recite by heart.

Saul took a deep breath and exhaled in frustration. "Oy vey, John. An asset has to be something real. Something tangible! A house is an asset. A farm is an asset. A plant is an asset. A factory is an asset. A shop is an asset. A business is an asset. But now Wall Street is claiming that a process can somehow be treated as though it were a real asset as well?"

"Yes, and for the reasons I just explained to you … CDOs— collateralized debt obligations—are backed by the values of the real assets you just mentioned … backed up by the values of the real assets that *underlie* them—"

"But CDOs are not real assets. They are paper derivatives!"

John turned away in frustration and started looking out the cabin window. "I don't understand what you mean by 'paper derivatives.'"

Saul waved his hand in the air before responding. "Son, to my old-fashioned way of thinking, you can't turn a process into a *security* without smoke and mirrors." He lowered his head, letting his glasses slip down his nose. "To my way of thinking, a debt, for example, can only be securitized by the *collateral* against which the bank lends the money! Because a house is a real asset, it can be used as the specific collateral against which the bank lends money. The bank holds onto the collateral as the buyer makes those monthly mortgage payments …"

John smiled politely. "So? What's your point?"

"But now, all of a sudden, you are telling me that the abstract *process* of people making their monthly mortgage payments can *itself* be collateralized as well? Doesn't make any sense!"

John looked annoyed. "It does too make sense! It makes sense because you start out by collateralizing those debt obligations—that's why they're called collateralized debt obligations!"

"Who says you can manipulate people's house payments like that? Who says the monthly mortgage payments that people are making on their private homes can be pooled, doctored, chopped up, sliced, manipulated, and mutilated in that way? Your 'syndicate'?"

John had to turn his face away.

Saul continued. "What was your 'syndicate' doing, John? Issuing ten dollars' worth of CDO paper derivatives backed up by one dollar's worth of real assets? What was the ratio? What were the numbers?"

John started laughing nervously. "Ratios? Numbers? Ah, I forgot. My dear father used to teach mathematics at Purdue."

"Yes, and your dear father says this whole CDO thing sounds like a Ponzi scheme!"

John had to protest angrily. "No, Papa! It definitely was not a Ponzi scheme."

"It wasn't?"

"No!"

"You're so sure of that? You're telling your dear father that CDOs are like a big box of anticipated monthly loan payments that can be mixed, pooled, chopped, inflated, and sliced up into real securities that can be bought, sold, traded—is that it?"

John nodded silently as he looked away.

Saul had to take another deep breath. He was obviously having a hard time reconciling what he was hearing with his own tried and true common sense. "Okay, John, okay. So who decides which of these casino chips—excuse me, collateralized debt obligations—are low risk and which are high risk?"

"The syndicate!"

Hearing again the word "syndicate," Saul ripped off his glasses in frustration. Already John had thrown a number of unfamiliar financial concepts at him, and he was starting to feel the weight of information overload. He would have liked to lose his temper and go stomping out of the room, but that was not possible in this case.

Somehow he managed to regain his composure. "Don't give me this spiel about the 'syndicate,' John! The *rating agencies* are the ones that decide which slices of these securities are good and which are bad ... ya?"

"Yes, Papa, you're absolutely right!"

"Rating agencies ... like Moody's and Standard & Poor's ... the same ones that rated Enron AAA, ya?"

"Yes, well, they're part of the syndicate too."

"The rating agencies are part of the syndicate?"

"Everybody's part of the syndicate."

Saul couldn't hold his temper any longer. He slapped the armchair rest with the palm of his hand and blurted out his next question. "And who in heaven's name was the flaming genius who convinced the rating agencies to grade some of these make-believe 'securities' AAA?"

John dismissed the question with a wave of his hand. "It wasn't me, Papa!"

Saul had to take a few more deep breaths, calm his nerves, and pause before continuing. "Well, I don't like what I'm hearing, John! It doesn't seem kosher to me!"

"What doesn't?"

"So *you* think it's kosher, do you? It's kosher to gamble with people's lives and fortunes like that? It's kosher to wave a magic wand, turn people's house payments into CDOs, derivatives, bet-to-fail shenanigans, and coffin trades that speculators can toy with? Does *that* sound kosher to you, boy?" The sarcasm in Saul's voice was beginning to turn into righteous indignation.

John turned his face away and waved his hands as though wanting to abdicate on grounds of fatigue and frustration.

But Saul wasn't about to relax his grip. "And tell me, boy, what happens when people get sick, or lose their jobs and can't make monthly payments? What happens when those 'anticipated' loan payments don't flow into your make-believe box anymore, eh?"

John was ready with the answer: "Those asset-backed securities would be put into the high-risk tranches!"

Saul had to take another deep breath, exhale, and try to collect himself. "Ya, okay, John. Let me try to understand what it was that led to the 2008 subprime mortgage meltdown. Basically, the meltdown happened because some coffin makers on Wall Street were conjuring up, leveraging, inflating, and peddling billions of dollars' worth of imaginary 'securities' that traders like my son could wager with, is that it?"

John remained silent, preferring not to say anything his father might interpret as an admission of guilt in his presently agitated state. He poured himself more champagne and gulped it down nervously.

Saul slapped the armchair rest with the palm of his hand again. "And, *who*, pray tell, *who* was the flaming genius who cooked up this whole CDO fantasy? Who was the *maven* who turned the American economy into a gambling parlor in which anything goes, including multibillion-dollar bet-to-fail shenanigans and coffin trades? And don't give me that spiel about 'the syndicate'!"

John had to turn his face away again. He seemed annoyed. "Don't look at me like that … it wasn't me!"

"Oh? It wasn't you? Well, I'm glad to hear that it wasn't you." Saul was being sarcastic again. "If it wasn't you, who was it? Some Nobel Laureate at the London School of Economics?"

John remained silent.

"Who was it? Tell me, boy! Was it some senator … like what I heard about … uh … what's his name … Phil Graham?"

John was quick with his answer. "Senator Phil Graham had something to do with deregulating the financial industry, but he wasn't the one who invented CDOs."

"Then who was it? Alan Greenspan? George Soros? Milton Friedman? Some flaming genius working at the Treasury? The Federal Reserve? The IMF? The World Bank? Who was it?"

"I'm guessing it was either some well-intentioned financial wizard working at Morgan, or maybe it was Joseph Lasagno," John replied, shrugging innocently, his face still turned away from his father.

"Joseph who?"

"Joseph Lasagno … you know, the guy working for Mega Assurance International Group."

Saul couldn't believe what he was hearing. "Let me get this straight. One man, working for a big insurance conglomerate, may have cooked up this toxic borscht all by himself? Is that what you're telling me? And the government, and the SEC, and the regulators, and the rating agencies, and your 'syndicate' let him get away with it?"

In the silence that ensued, Saul realized he was behaving like an attorney badgering the witness and decided to back off a little. He started laughing. "Joe Lasagno cooked up CDOs all by himself, did he? Oy! Joe should've stayed in the kitchen and cooked up lasagna instead! Maybe then there wouldn't have been a global financial meltdown to begin with!"

"Yes, well, like I said, it wasn't me!" John was starting to feel the cabin walls closing in on him. And the generous glasses of champagne he had imbibed were beginning to have their effect as well. "I was just following the rules. Okay?"

Saul had to take a moment to calm down. In his agitated state his glasses had slid down his nose again, and he had to push them back up and readjust them. He looked down at the list that he had brought along with him before continuing.

"Okay, John, here's my next question for you. I want to know all about *MBSs—mortgaged-backed securities*. What are they? Different kinds of CDOs? Someone told me you became a billionaire overnight betting against mortgage-backed securities ... explain mortgage-backed securities to me!"

John couldn't help tensing up anew. The words "mortgage-backed securities" had struck a nerve connected to some Gordian Knot of guilt and responsibility, it seemed. "Well, yes, that's more or less correct ... umm, I made a lot of money betting against mortgage-backed securities when I realized some of them had been incorrectly rated as low risk."

"Incorrectly rated low risk? By whom? Your 'syndicate'?"

"By the rating agencies—"

"And that's when you went and bet against the American dream, ya? That's when you made your historic wager against people's houses and homes, ya?"

"No, Papa, that's not quite correct!"

"No? Then what exactly did you do if you didn't bet against the American dream?"

John had to put on a humble face before answering. "Well, unlike a whole lot of other people in the government, unlike a whole lot of other people on Wall Street and in the rating agencies, I did my homework! A lot of homework! And I paid my team a lot of money to do some of the homework as well."

"Homework, eh? I should be proud of my son for doing his homework."

"Yes! We did our homework and discovered that a whole lot of people had been 'gifted' with mortgages they couldn't afford—"

"Gifted? By whom? Your 'syndicate'?"

"Well, actually, by the government ... you know, Fannie Mae and Freddie Mac ... you've heard of them no doubt?"

Saul had previously Googled Fannie Mae and Freddie Mac and couldn't help breaking out in sarcastic laughter again. "Ah yes, ladies and gentlemen! Fannie and Freddie of *Alice in Wonderland* fame! Twiddle Dee and Twiddle Dum, dancing gleefully as they drained the American taxpayer of untold billions of dollars! And where, pray tell, *where* in heaven's name was the Mad Hatter in all this?"

John looked annoyed. "C'mon, Papa, that's not funny!"

Saul stopped laughing and put on his serious face again. "So tell me, boy, why on earth would the government want to gift people with mortgages they can't afford?"

John turned his face and shrugged again. "I don't know ... in order to enable them to share in the American dream of home ownership, I suppose."

"Even if they can't afford it?"

John knew his father to be a staunch conservative and didn't want to get into arguments about the morality or immorality of government handouts. "Well, whatever the motive may have been, the fact was, a whole lot of people ended up with subprime mortgages they couldn't afford, mortgages they were bound to default on sooner or later ..."

"And you saw all this coming and you jumped on it?"

"Well, like I said, we did our homework and discovered a flaw in the system."

"A flaw in the system?"

John abruptly sat up, realizing he may have let slip more than necessary. He tried to change the subject. "Well, I wasn't the one that made the rules, was I?" His words sounded somewhat incoherent, and he had to gulp down more champagne to steady his nerves.

"You saw a flaw in the system and exploited it for all it was worth. That's it, isn't it?" Saul seemed to have gotten the admission of guilt that he was after.

John could do nothing but turn away and repeat himself. "Like I said, my team and I did a lot of hard work ... we dug deep and discovered the existence of a whole lot of mortgage-backed securities that weren't worth the paper they were written on ..."

"So you went and *shorted* the whole lot, ya?"

"I took huge financial risks! I bet a lot of money against incorrectly rated mortgage-backed securities ... yes ... and when they did actually default, I made a lot of money overnight."

"Tens of billions of dollars in a couple of weeks, ya?"

"Yes, well, I did nothing illegal and nothing improper. I was just following the rules!"

Saul listened with amazement. "You were one of the rare people who saw the housing bubble about to burst and didn't raise an alarm that might have prevented a global economic catastrophe—because you wanted to cash in on it, ya?"

John sat up nervously and started fidgeting with the edge of the armchair rest. He rudely blurted his next words. "Well, it wasn't just me, was it? Other people were doing the same thing! The signs were all over the place ... anyone with half a brain could've seen the housing bubble about to burst."

Saul looked amazed. "And where were the government regulators in all this?"

John's head jerked back in disbelief as he looked at his father in astonishment. "Government regulators? What a joke! Ha ha ha ha! Very funny! Government regulators! They had no idea what was going on."

Saul looked more disgusted than ever. He loved his son, flesh of his flesh, but this whole thing seemed bigger than both of them. He tried to force a smile born of fatherly compassion, but the smile was short lived. "Okay, son, okay ... fine! You did your homework. You followed the rules. You saw a flaw in the system. You discovered that a whole lot of subprime mortgages weren't worth the paper they were written on. You started some sort of a hedge fund. You called up your rich friends. You all pooled your money, leveraged your capital or whatever, and purchased billions of dollars' worth of worthless subprime mortgage-backed securities. You then *shorted* them and made billions of dollars in a couple of weeks, ya? Is that it, more or less?"

John seemed more nervous than ever. He paused to pour himself more champagne and took his time answering. "Well, not quite."

"Not quite? What do you mean, not quite? They tell me yours was one of the biggest coffin trades in the history of Wall Street!"

John put down the champagne glass, leaned over to squarely face his father, and then responded slowly and rudely. "I didn't exactly *short* them." He sounded like a lawyer asking a judge to dismiss a case on a technicality.

"What? You didn't *short* them? Then how on earth did you get rich betting against billions of dollars of mortgage-backed securities?" Saul sounded more incredulous than ever. He laughed again and shook his head.

John leaned back. "I did so by means of *credit-default swaps* ..." His words were muffled and sounded shifty.

"Credit-default swaps?"

"Yes! Credit-default swaps—CDSs ... no doubt you've heard of them? No doubt it's one of the things you've written on that interrogation list you brought with you—*on our vacation to Bermuda?*"

Saul looked sad. He started rocking back and forth in his armchair again. "Aha, I see! I see! I get it now! My clever son did his homework, connected all the dots, saw a flaw in the system, exploited it for all it was worth, and made billions of dollars betting against the American dream. And, mind you ... my clever son did all of this, not by short trades or put options but by credit-default swaps! I should be proud of my son! I should take out a full-page ad in the *Wall Street Journal* telling the whole world how proud I am of my son."

John had to turn away again. "I don't know what it is that you are accusing me of." His voice sounded weak and faint. He put his head to the cold glass of the cabin window and began to survey the serenity and peacefulness of the sky and clouds that passed silently below them.

Saul, however, was relentless. "Okay, boy, okay! Now please explain CDSs—credit-default swaps to me. Tell your father what they are and how you used them in your ribald wager against the American dream."

John gave his father another angry look and then turned away to press his face against the cold window again. He mumbled something.

Saul raised his hand to his right ear. "Speak up, boy, I can't hear you."

John turned to face his father again before answering rudely. "Insurance policy! Think of a credit-default swap as an insurance policy, okay?" He turned away again.

"Insurance policy? Insurance against what?"

"Insurance against credit defaults—what else?"

Saul seemed taken aback. "So a credit-default swap is supposed to be some sort of insurance that speculators can take out to protect themselves in case other people default on the mortgages they can't afford? Is that it?"

John nodded weakly.

"Then why call it a credit-default *swap*?" Why not be honest about the whole thing and call it credit-default *insurance*?"

"Well … because … in case people default on their mortgages, the holder of the credit-default swap can go to the insurance provider and swap it for cash."

"Swap it for cash? Really! What else would you want to swap it for? Seashells? Beads? Wampum?"

"That's not funny." John looked more annoyed than ever. "I admit it's a kind of a misnomer … but on Wall Street and elsewhere they started calling it credit-default swaps and that's what we're stuck with, so there."

Saul sat up and began to smile fiendishly. "Let me take a guess! The real reason they didn't call it credit-default *insurance* was to avoid insurance regulations! They called it credit-default *swaps* so Wall Street could buy dirt cheap housing bubble insurance without the insurers actually having to back up their policies with adequate reserves! Yes, by golly, that's it, isn't it? And of course when the housing bubble burst, the taxpayer ended up having to bail out the insurers so the insurers could pay off their Wall Street clients! Feh! What a way to swindle and rob the taxpayer!"

John took another sip of champagne and swallowed loudly. Dom Pérignon and his father's questions were beginning to make him groggy.

Saul was relentless. "Okay, so let me get this straight: you're telling me that *anyone*—any speculator on Wall Street—can go take out credit-default insurance against other people's mortgages, is that it? And when other people default on their mortgages, the speculator can go to the 'insurance provider' and swap the piece of paper for cash?"

John was silent.

Saul seemed enraged. He slapped the armchair rest with his hand again before continuing: "And *who*, pray tell, *who* was the flaming genius who went and cooked up these credit-default swaps now?"

John was quick with his answer. "I think it was Joe Lasagno … or at least he was the one who revived the whole thing."

"Joe Lasagno … again?" Saul couldn't help breaking into laughter again. He slapped his thigh with his right hand as though feigning Mark

Twain humor. "There you have it, ladies and gents! The same coffin maker who conjured up casino chips in the form of collateralized-debt obligations then went and invented credit-default swaps to insure against gambling losses. Yessiree, Bob! Like moths to the flame, like flies to the honey, there's nothing like a sure bet to attract speculators to Wall Street."

John had to interrupt. "Well, like I said, it wasn't me. I did nothing improper, okay? I just did my homework, took huge financial risks, followed the rules, and made a lot of money for my clients! Is there a law against that?"

"You're so sure you did nothing wrong—is that it?"

"I'm sure I didn't violate any laws."

Saul seemed saddened and taken aback. He lowered his voice before continuing. "Well, son, you may not have violated any man-made laws, but there are higher laws to be considered here! Proverbs 29:24 tells us—"

"Aha! I knew it." John was quick to cut his father off. He abruptly sat up, rolled his eyes, and smiled triumphantly. "Higher laws? Now we're going to talk about God, aren't we?" He waved his hand as though to dismiss an undesirable subject without further ado, but then quieted down and bowed his head in frustration. "What are you handing me, Papa? What did I get myself into? A relaxing vacation to Bermuda? Or a tzedakah lecture?"

Saul responded slowly, and with sadness in his voice. "So now my son has something against tzedakah? I should be proud of my son!"

John turned away again before blurting out his next words. "I don't want to get into it with you." He waved his hand in the air again. "We've been through this whole subject time and again ... I don't want to talk about it now."

Saul had to calm down, reach over, and put his hand on his son's shoulder. "Yes, I know. I understand. Of course you don't want to talk about it ... we've been through all of this before ... you believe the existence of God to be incompatible with the horrors of the Holocaust."

John responded weakly with his face still turned away. "Yes, well, I've put the question to you before, haven't I? And you've *never* given me a satisfactory answer!" The way in which John blurted out the word never caused Saul to draw farther back. "You want to tell me now, Papa? You want to explain it to me now? Where was your 'God' when the Nazis were gassing Grandpa Mordecai and Grandma Rivka at Dachau?"

Saul didn't know what to say. It took him a moment or two to recover. He responded with his voice lowered. "Nevertheless, John … nevertheless, we are Jews. We are supposed to be righteous … that's a beautiful thing. If we lose that … what is there left?"

John's response was immediate. "I didn't ask to be born a Jew, did I?" His words sounded crass and insensitive. He backed away in the sudden realization that he had deeply hurt his father. He lowered his voice and bowed his head. "The last time I was in temple I was thirteen years old … I gave a speech and received thirty-eight fountain pens … I have enough fountain pens, thank you … I don't need anymore."

He turned away and pressed his face against the cold glass again. "I don't want to talk about it … as far as I'm concerned, there are no higher laws … we're governed by man-made laws, and I'm not guilty of violating any of them … so what's my sin? What are you accusing me of?" His breath fogged up part of the window.

But Saul wasn't about to give up. "Okay. You've convinced yourself you've done nothing wrong. You're as pure as the driven snow, is that it?"

John looked overly pressed and irritated. He seemed to be on the verge of tears. He turned to face his father again. "Just tell me what it is you're accusing me of! Whatever it is, get it off your chest so we can enjoy our vacation together."

Saul had to take a few moments to calm down and gather his thoughts before answering. "Do you remember when you were small and I would take you fishing on that lake?"

John suddenly found himself relaxing and smiling. "Yes, those were happy days, weren't they? We didn't catch too many fish, but we sure had a lot of fun together, didn't we?"

Saul had to relax and smile as well. "Yes we did. We did indeed, son."

John sat up enthusiastically. "Wait till you see what I've arranged for us in Bermuda. I've chartered a big boat just for the two of us. We're going fishing, Papa! We are going hunting for blue marlin."

Saul seemed genuinely surprised and momentarily excited but then returned to the grim reality of the subject at hand. "Do you remember how you used to throw stones into the lake … the circular ripples expanding outward?"

John continued smiling. "Yes, I remember throwing stones into the lake ... and I remember you trying to explain the mathematics of those expanding circles."

Saul started rocking back and forth in his armchair again. "Let me explain what you recently did on Wall Street. You threw a boulder the size of a house into that little lake, generating tidal waves that altered the geography and topography of the entire shoreline."

It took a moment for John to realize what his father was getting at. He sank into his chair. "What are you saying?"

"You know exactly what I'm saying."

"No, I don't!"

Saul leaned over to put his hand on John's shoulder again and looked into his eyes. "Son, don't you understand that what you did on Wall Street caused adverse reactions in markets worldwide?"

John tried to assume an air of indifference. "So? Didn't you once tell me even the flap of a butterfly's wing can cause a reaction in the world? You're a mathematician ... you should know that—"

"We're not talking about butterfly wings, we're talking about a multibillion-dollar coffin trade that contributed to economic meltdowns all over the world ... millions of families lost their homes, John. Millions of breadwinners lost their jobs, their life savings ... couldn't feed their kids anymore ... their lives were turned upside down!"

John was still indifferent. "Well, I put my own life and fortune on the line as well! I took *huge* financial risks; isn't that what an entrepreneur does? I did my homework, I operated within the rules, and I made a lot of money for my grateful clients ... what's wrong with that?"

Saul had to remove his hand from John's shoulder. "You still don't get it, do you? What's wrong with you, boy? Do your mind and conscience fail you? Did I do such a lousy job raising you?"

John turned away again.

Saul continued. "What is it that George Soros calls it? *Reflexivity?*"

John turned to face his father again. He looked surprised and amused. "Reflexivity? Never heard of it."

"Really. Well, allow me to explain it to you." Saul pushed his glasses back up the bridge of his nose and began reading words he had scribbled on the piece of paper that he had brought along with him. "Reflexivity describes a self-reinforcing feedback mechanism driven by changing market expectations."

John had to laugh. "Ah, I forgot again! My father used to teach mathematics at Purdue University. So, professor, please do explain what those words mean."

"They mean this: when my clever son bet billions of dollars against mortgage-backed securities, he helped set into motion a self-fulfilling prophecy."

"How so?"

"My son bet billions of dollars against mortgage-backed securities he knew weren't worth the paper they were written on. The word got around and other people on Wall Street started asking questions: 'Why is this guy betting billions against mortgage-backed securities? Does he know something we don't?' Soon other people started betting against mortgage-backed securities. Before you knew it, every speculator was betting against mortgage-backed securities. The bets augmented one another ... the negative expectations reinforced the downward spiral ... and soon the process became irreversible."

"Yes, okay, very eloquent! But where can you fault *me* specifically? 'Be specific!' Isn't that what you've always told me? Now I'm asking you to 'be specific': what's my sin?"

"You still don't get the big picture, do you? Let me spell it out for you. Some coffin maker working for a mega-insurance conglomerate chops up peoples' mortgages into bags of straw called CDOs, auctions them off to pyromaniacs, and then sells those same pyromaniacs dirt-cheap fire insurance in the form of credit-default swaps! And no one understands why the whole thing had to go up in flames? No one understands why the taxpayers were asked to bail out the 'too big to fail' mega-insurers that were peddling dirt-cheap fire insurance to pyromaniacs?"

"What are you accusing me of now? Arson?"

"No, son, you didn't light the match yourself ... you only invested in billions of dollars' worth of straw mortgages, purchased dirt-cheap fire insurance, and then just sat around waiting for lightning to strike."

"Bravo, Papa, how poetic! But you still haven't answered my question: What's my *specific* sin in all this?"

"You bet against people's houses! You helped turn people's homes and life savings into so much goat droppings!" Saul's anger had suddenly returned, as evidenced by pulsating veins in his neck.

John had to protest strongly. "No! That's not what I did! I just followed the rules of the game. Rules are rules. If you don't like the rules, then go and take it up with the rule makers."

"And who might that be?"

"The syndicate!"

"Again with the syndicate?" Saul ripped off his glasses. "Who in heaven's name is this syndicate?"

"I told you: it's everybody!"

"You mean everybody on Wall Street?"

"No! I mean everybody—including you."

"Don't be silly, boy. I'm not a member of your syndicate."

"Yes you are."

Saul threw up his hands in frustration and took a deep breath. "Now you've completely lost me. You've gone mad. Wall Street has made my son go crazy!"

John continued, but now with a more sober and measured tone of voice. "You are as much a member of the syndicate as anyone else, Papa. You are a citizen. You vote. You pay taxes. Like it or lump it, you are a member of the syndicate,"

"What *are* you talking about, boy?"

"I'm talking about *democracy*, Papa!" John shouted out the words.

Saul was taken aback. "Democracy?"

"Yes—you've heard of it? 'Government of the people, by the people, for the people—'"

"Don't give me history lessons, boy!" It was now Saul's turn to be rude.

A long silence ensued.

John continued his sober diatribe. "If you're looking for someone to blame, go blame the American people."

Saul sat up abruptly. "Really! And why would I want to blame the American people for something *you* did?"

"Because they were the ones who allowed it."

"And why would they allow coffin trades like yours on Wall Street?"

"Because they're too stupid to know otherwise."

John's words angered Saul. He slapped the armchair rest with the palm of his hand again. "Don't you *ever* talk about the American people like that again. This is the greatest nation on earth, founded on Judeo-Christian principles. Why, if Governor William Bradford had had his way, Hebrew would be the official second language being taught in all American schools."

John knew his father to be a great admirer of America's founders and Constitution and didn't want to give him the opportunity to start preaching on that score. "Yes, I know, Papa, I know! This is a great country—land of hope and glory."

The sarcasm in John's voice angered Saul even more, and he had to take a moment to calm himself. "The American people are not stupid, John. They may be ill-informed about Wall Street's bet-to-fail shenanigans and coffin trades ... but they're not stupid. They're just busy!"

"Busy doing what?"

"Raising their kids. Running their businesses. Working their fingers to the bone. Working from sunrise to sunset. Working from cradle to grave. That's why they hire politicians to go to Washington and do for them what they are too busy to do for themselves."

"Then go blame the politicians."

Silence ensued. They sat pensively in the luxurious interior of the corporate jet, listening to the muffled sound of the outside air rushing by at five hundred mph.

Saul was the one to break the silence. He spoke with a lowered voice, and what he had to say took John by surprise: "You know, son ... I might agree with you."

"About what?"

"About who the real culprits may be in all this craziness."

"Who?"

"The politicians—who else? The civil servants the American people have hired to go do for them what they are too busy to do for themselves."

"Yes, well, like I said, I just follow the rules. If you don't like the rules, then go blame the politicians."

There was a certain amount of logic in John's defense and Saul had to calm down completely. "This reminds me of an ancient Hebrew saying: 'A hole in the fence encourages the thief!'"

"Meaning what?"

"In ancient Israel, people were responsible for building and maintaining protective fences around their homes and farms. If there was a hole in the fence, it was the solemn duty of the householder to fix it. If the householder was too lazy to fix the hole in the fence, encouraging a thief to enter and steal things, then the householder was blameworthy."

"Yes, well, there you have it! Today's politicians are either too lazy or too stupid to fix the hole in the fence. They're too busy handing out pork, voting themselves raises, and worrying about reelection. Stop blaming me and go blame them. Or better yet, go blame the American people for putting up with incompetent politicians in the first place."

Saul seemed momentarily humbled by his son's reasoning. "Okay, John, okay. Point well taken! So what do you suggest?"

"About what?"

"About fixing the hole in the fence. You of all people have 'been there, done that,' and you are in a good position to know how to fix the hole in the fence. Suppose you were the president of the United States, voted into office by the American people, and given a mandate to restore dignity to Wall Street. How would you go about doing it? How would you put an end to all the bet-to-fail shenanigans and coffin trades? How would you deal with the dark side of Wall Street?"

"The dark side of Wall Street? Is there a light side?"

"Of course there is. Everything on Wall Street isn't run by the dark side of the force. Most of Wall Street is powered by honest, hardworking American free enterprise."

John seemed genuinely surprised. "I didn't know my dear father was so optimistic about Wall Street. Sorry, Papa, American free enterprise is no match for the dark side of the force. As Darth Vader once said to Luke Skywalker, 'You don't know the power of the dark side!'"

Saul laughed and seemed comfortable in going along with the *Star Wars* theme. "Hah! I should be proud of my son, the Sith lord! But if my memory serves me right, Luke Skywalker eventually destroyed the Sith and converted his father!"

Now it was John's turn to laugh. "So now I'm Darth Vader? And you're ... what? Yoda? Sorry, Yoda! It's too late. The whole thing is hopeless!"

The two continued laughing, but Saul had to put on a serious face again. "Answer the question, John. If you were the president, what would you do? How would my son go about restoring dignity to the American economy?"

John seemed humbled and honored by his father's question and didn't know what to say. He reached forward to pour himself more champagne but then stopped, withdrew, and leaned back. "What would I do, as president?"

"Yes, what would you do?"

"I would urge the American people to wake up from the sleep of the dead, fire the incompetent politicians, and hire public servants who will roll up their sleeves and fix the hole in the fence."

"And what would that entail, specifically? Be specific."

"Well, for starters, they would have to fix the hole in the Dodd-Frank[3] legislation."

"Fix Dodd-Frank? Why, what's wrong with it?"

"It's toothless!"

"So how would *you* fix it, Mr. President?"

"I would put real teeth in it."

"How so?" Saul seemed fascinated by what he was hearing.

"I would … I would shut down the ISDA—"

"ISDA? What's that?"

"International Swaps and Derivatives Association."

"Sounds like an elite club, John!"

"Yes, elite … and very powerful. I'm a member myself!"

Saul had to gulp down hard. "Oy! I should be proud of my son, a Sith lord."

John couldn't help laughing perversely.

Saul continued. "Can the ISDA be shut down?"

John had to think before answering. "It wouldn't be easy … but it could be done by the president of the United States."

"And what would shutting down the ISDA accomplish?"

---

[3] The Dodd-Frank Act refers to the Wall Street Reform and Consumer Protection Act of 2010 authored by Senator Chris Dodd and Representative Barney Frank pursuant to the financial crisis of 2007–10. It was intended to bring about a sweeping overhaul of the US financial regulatory system, but some critics have attacked it as not going far enough to avoid similar financial meltdowns.

"Well, it would put an end to most of your 'coffin trades' … and that's what you want, isn't it?"

Saul had to take a deep breath before continuing. "Ya, okay, Mr. President, so you would shut down the ISDA … what else would you do to restore sanity to Wall Street?"

"What else would I do? I'd immediately reinstate the Glass-Steagall firewall,[4] prohibiting commercial banks from engaging in speculation." John gave himself a righteous nod of approval and smiled at his father.

Saul was dumfounded. He started beaming with pride all of a sudden. "Yes! Very good! Go on, go on. What else would you do?"

John couldn't help waxing righteous. "As the nation's chief executive, I would cut an order declaring the trillions of dollars in outstanding credit-default swaps be made null, void, and worthless."

Saul was speechless. John's words seemed to have knocked him for a loop. He seemed genuinely enthused and amazed. "Oy! I was mistaken! My son is no Sith lord. My son is a high-ranking member of the Jedi council."

John continued. "But that's not going to happen, is it, Papa?"

"Why not?"

"Because, for starters, someone would have to go and wake up the American people from the sleep of the dead." There was a note of despair in John's words.

"And you don't think that's possible?"

"No, I don't think that's possible. I think the whole thing is hopeless."

Saul shook his head. "I didn't know you were such a pessimist. I should

---

[4] The Glass-Steagall Act refers to the Banking Act of 1933 authored by Senator Carter Glass and Representative Henry B. Steagall. Four of the provisions of the Glass-Steagall Act were designed to be preemptive in nature and had the effect of erecting as it were a protective wall of separation, or "firewall," between the traditional/respectable activities of banks and the questionable/speculative activities of Wall Street. By repealing the germane provisions of the Glass-Steagall Act, the Gramm-Leach-Bliley Act of 1999 (sponsored by Senator Phil Gramm, and representatives Jim Leach and Thomas J. Bliley) had the effect of removing the Glass-Steagall "firewall," thereby opening the floodgates to the advent of questionable and often toxic financial instruments such as the Mortgage-Backed Security (MBS), the Collateralized Debt Obligation (CDO), and the Credit-Default Swap (CDS).

be proud of my son! My son likes to go through life spreading sunshine all around."

"Sorry, but there's no sunshine to spread. No blue sky over the horizon, only dark clouds. Like I said, the whole thing is hopeless."

Saul did his best to put on a cheerful smile. "Or, maybe, just maybe, it's not so hopeless? Maybe, with a little help from above, the American people can be roused to proper action?"

John rolled his eyes again. "Yes, well, mazel tov with that idea. And now we're going to talk about God again, aren't we? Sorry, but I don't think even Moses and Elijah could wake the American people from the sleep of the dead."

"Why not?"

"It's called *inertia*."

"Inertia?"

"Yes, inertia ... *an object at rest will remain at rest from now until doomsday unless acted upon by some external force.*"

Saul looked annoyed. "Don't give me science lessons, boy. I know all about inertia. But I still think you're wrong! I think the sleeping giant is finally beginning to stir. And, ironically, your coffin trade may have had something to do with it."

"Really?"

"Yes! What was it Yamamoto said?"

"Yamamoto? Who's he?"

"He was the Japanese admiral who wasn't very happy about Pearl Harbor. While other Japanese leaders were claiming a great victory there, Yamamoto was fearful about the final outcome. Do you remember what he said?"

"What did he say?"

"He said, 'I fear all we have done is to awaken a sleeping giant and fill him with a terrible resolve.'"

"Interesting, but what does that have to do with—"

"Your coffin trade may have been the Pearl Harbor needed to wake up the sleeping giant!"

"Very poetic, Papa, but I wouldn't bet on it."

"Well, I for one, *would* be willing to bet on it."

John was quick to take up his father's offer. "You're on."

"And if I win?" Saul couldn't help smiling.

"If you win, I'll probably drop dead with surprise. But if I don't drop dead first, I promise I'll stop being an agnostic and become an orthodox believer like you."

"Just like that? You'd stop being an agnostic and start believing in God? Why?"

"Because in my opinion, *only* God could wake the American people from the sleep of the dead. So if the American people do actually wake up from the sleep of the dead, that'll be a sure sign God exists."

Saul seemed genuinely touched by his son's logic. He held out his arm and the two shook hands.

Just then the smart-looking stewardess in the chic uniform entered the cabin again to serve father and son fancy hors d'oeuvres made with the world's most expensive caviar, and to announce that the jet was going to land in Bermuda in about twenty-five minutes.

John poured his father more champagne, and they raised their glasses in a toast. "May the force be with us," John said, smiling at his father.

Saul preferred the more traditional Jewish toast: "L'chaim!"

Chapter 2

Bad Money:
A Down and Dirty Narrative

Of all the foul growths currently in the world, the worst is money.
Money drives men from home, plunders proud cities, and
perverts honest minds to shameful practice, godlessness
and crime.—Sophocles, *Antigone*

The history of money is a down and dirty narrative. Greek philosophers wrote about the misuses of money, such as Sophocles lamenting its power to destroy cities and men. The echoes of Virgil's words, *auri sacra fames* ("the accursed lust for gold")[5] has panged the conscience of man throughout the ages. The words of the Roman orator Cicero, "There is no fortress so strong that money cannot take it"[6] rings as true in the US Congress today as it did in the Roman senate twenty centuries ago. Twenty centuries ago Christ fashioned a whip and used it to drive the moneychangers out of the temple (John 2:15). In his letter to Timothy, St. Paul placed the love of money at the root of all kinds of evil (1 Timothy 6:10).

Listen carefully and you may hear the words of Sir Thomas Gresham

---

[5] Man's appetite for gold can be said to be ancient and insatiable. In his epic poem *Aeneid*, the Roman poet Virgil wrote of *auri sacra fames* ("the accursed lust for gold") and the spiritual wretchedness associated with it.

[6] Marcus Tullius Cicero, *In Verrem*, listed in *The Great Quotations*, compiled by George Seldes (New York: Pocket Books, 1976), 605.

resonating in the world's financial markets even today: "Bad money drives out good."[7]

Much of human literature revolves around the down and dirty aspect of money. Great writers such as Chaucer, Shakespeare, Dickens, Dante, Milton, Whitman, Beckett, Twain, and Dostoevsky seized on the theme to weave tales of pride and prejudice, greed and impropriety, scandal and dishonor, graft and corruption, bribery and extortion, blackmail and iniquity, shame and disgrace, indignity and injustice, power and corruption, tales about tyrants and slaves, oppressors and oppressed, haves and have-nots. Karl Marx's *Das Kapital* was the prelude to anarchy, chaos, communism, violence, and death on a global scale.

Capitalism itself has been a bumpy ride, to say the least. In America the money-driven stock market crash of 1929 was the prelude to the breadlines and soup kitchens of the Great Depression. And there have been endless cycles of booms and busts ever since. Bulls and bears. Upturns and downturns. A brief period of prosperity, followed by a period of recession. Up and down. Up and down.

It would be an understatement to say the United States is now facing the greatest financial crisis in her history. It is a crisis of such magnitude that there are no precedents to be found for it anywhere. Today, America's annual deficits are many times greater than the total federal expenditures of the first two hundred years of the Republic! And as federal spending outdistances taxes, the difference must be met with more borrowing, which means even more deficits!

During the 1950s President Eisenhower demanded to be notified if even twelve banks were on the FDIC's troubled list. If he were to come back to life, he would go into shock upon being notified about the number now on that list and the number that have already failed. No doubt Ike would have called for a state of national emergency when informed about the nation's deficits. He would have had a heart attack and retired back to

---

[7] Attributed to the English financier Sir Thomas Gresham (1519–79), also referred to as "Gresham's Law," which predicts that bad money will tend to drive out good money. Applied to the contemporary world of Wall Street, Gresham's Law would have predicted that junk bonds, derivatives, collateralized-debt obligations, mortgage-backed securities, credit-default swaps, and other toxic financial instruments would eventually drive out sound money, traditional capital, and wise investment.

heaven when confronted with the recent subprime mortgage meltdown. His dying words would no doubt have been, "How did this happen?"

We need to pause, take a deep breath, obtain a proper perspective, and ask ourselves the same question: "How did all this happen?"

Although America has advanced beyond the wildest dreams of Adam Smith in terms of the diversification of trades, and specialization of skills and divisions of labor, American free enterprise languishes and the wealth-creating genius of the nation remains shackled to the quotas of some bizarre monetary expedient dating back to the seventeenth century. "How did this happen?"

With all the cutbacks and belt-tightening, there doesn't seem to be any end to *systemic* price inflation! In spite of a sluggish economy, in spite of the fact that untold billions of dollars are being retired from circulation annually in payment of interest, and in spite of an ever-growing trade deficit that has the effect of siphoning many more billions out of the arteries of the US economy, *general* prices continue to rise inexorably and inexplicably, as though in defiance of the laws of gravity. "How did this happen?"

The specter of a gargantuan public debt hangs over the heads of unborn Americans like a hangman's noose. As of this writing the national debt of the United States has surpassed the *$16 trillion* mark. It is said that sixteen trillion one-dollar bills placed end to end would pave a four-lane highway all the way to the sun and back. Figures don't lie, and these figures underlie compound processes that are only now beginning to achieve critical mass. "How did this happen?"

The picture isn't much better elsewhere in the world. In August 1982 the government of Mexico announced it had run out of foreign exchange reserves and could not pay its debts. That announcement marked the beginning of a global monetary crisis that seems determined to unravel the economic structure of the entire planet. In 1980 that structure suffered the collapse of the Japanese housing bubble. Between 1980 and 1990 it suffered the spasms of the American Savings and Loan Crisis. In 1992–93 it was the European currency crisis. In 1997–98 the Asian currency crisis. In 1998, the Russian currency crisis. In the same year it witnessed the collapse and taxpayer bailout of Long-Term Capital Management (LTCM). In 2000 it was the collapse of the dot-com bubble. In 2001 the spectacular collapse of Enron. As of this writing, global economies are still reeling from the effects of the 2008 subprime mortgage meltdown. Greece, Spain, Portugal, France, Italy and a number of other European countries are teetering on the edge of economic chaos. "How did all this happen?"

To say economic uncertainty has become the watchword of our day would be a great understatement. Yet to these unprecedented woes, the so-called "experts" continue to apply assumptions, principles, axioms, and rules that are by now obsolete. Insanity has been defined as doing the same thing over and over and expecting different results. You can't fix something that's broken on the basis of the same set of assumptions that broke it in the first place—you will bounce off the same walls and end up right back where you started. America has been bouncing off the same walls for many decades.

Bad money can no longer be confined to territorial boundaries of nations. It travels the world on devil's wings, tearing asunder the fabric of human economies, and with it, the lives and fortunes of multiplied millions created in the image of God. Bad money not only drives out good money, it drives out good morals! Bad money stifles upright government. Bad money stifles free enterprise, wealth creation, prosperity, progress, and the general well being of which human civilization is capable. Bad money encourages speculators to cash in on chaos and profit from crisis. Bad money encourages investment bankers to privatize gain and socialize loss. Bad money encourages Wall Street to set a table of fortune for itself in the US Congress, the White House, and the Treasury.

Meanwhile on Main Street, bad money competes against the labor of man and tries to deprive him of the dignity of his origins in God. The cities of America are teetering on the edge of bankruptcy, covered with refuse and graffiti! They have become cesspools of congestion and waste, revolving doors of crime through which the indigent, the penniless, the rudderless, the disillusioned, the disenfranchised, and the homeless traffic on their way to the gray walls and cold watchtowers of San Quentin, Soledad, and Folsom. "How did this happen?"

The plant is shut down, the schoolhouse is empty, and the plow is left in mid-furrow, all for the privation of good money, the lack of which paralyzes all true progress, the lack of which has now become the stumbling block of living itself. In the wealthiest nation on earth we are faced with poverty of soul, living hand to mouth, living but to work and working but to live, as though money was the only occasion of a wearisome life, and a wearisome life the only occasion of money. "How did this happen?"

Schoolchildren need more teachers, but there isn't enough good money to hire them. Hospitals need more physicians, but there isn't enough good money to hire them. Cities need more peace officers, but there isn't enough good money to hire them. Environs are polluted, but there isn't enough good money to clean them up. Roads are falling apart, but there isn't enough good money to upgrade them. Bridges are falling apart, but there isn't enough good money to fix them. Dams and levies are falling apart, but there isn't enough good money to shore them up. Transit systems are falling apart, but there isn't enough good money to renovate them. Underground utilities, water pipes, sewage pipes, and electrical conduits are falling apart, but there isn't enough good money to renew them.

"How did this happen?"

Personal bankruptcies have reached epidemic proportions. On the heels of every hope looms the threat of default and mortgage foreclosure. Middle-class salaries are slashed. Pension plans are looted. Budgets are cut. The unemployment lines stretch from Maine to California. Millions are living below the poverty line. The widow and the orphan are left out in the cold. The poor and needy go hungry. The sick cannot afford physicians. The laborer can no longer put away a ransom for old age—the dream of the golden years has been replaced by a nightmare of poverty and the gloom of the geriatric ward!

"How did all this happen?"

Privation of the American Dream

Now, it was thought, with a great deal of certainty, that organized error had been dealt its death blow in the course of the American Revolution. And indeed, it was a great blow that America's founders were able to deliver into the ribcage of state-sanctioned iniquity. Unfortunately what was not and could not have been foreseen by them was the degree to which the ancient conflict would soon change its outward disguise and begin assuming an economic character. They did not—and could not—have foreseen the extent of the industrial and technological changes in the offing and the degree to which the *economy* would replace military might in order of importance as an essential condition of liberty and guarantee of peace.

Whereas the former disguises of iniquity are now footnotes to history, there is still one more disguise that has to be stripped before the proverbial beast can be laid to rest. This last disguise has to do with the issue of *money creation*.

For too long the issue of money creation has been left ill-defined and unresolved, to this day regarded as an occult science hidden behind a cloud of mystery and technical jargon. Otherwise intelligent Americans do not seem to know how their nation is being "financed," or who it is that creates new money, or by what system, or at what cost. Americans for the most part cannot explain why good money seems to be so scarce nowadays, or why the nation is now facing bankruptcy, saddled with a debt that is literally undergoing astronomical increases by the minute. They are at a loss as to why contradictions such as debt, poverty, and insecurity should be found in such proportions in the most God-blessed, abundant, and generous land on earth, or why such things as "recessions" should ever have to occur here in the first place! Needless to say, this is an appalling condition for people to find themselves in.

Perhaps one reason for this appalling condition has to do with the fact that the real problem is well camouflaged! The real problem lies in the three-hundred-year-old *system* of money creation itself, and not in the *methods* by which that system is administered. Our system of money creation is traceable to a seventeenth-century scaffolding of central banking that is now collapsing under the weight of its own convolution. That's the real problem.

Recall that for fifteen hundred years scholars kept making adjustments to Ptolemy's model of the earth-centered universe until in the end it collapsed under the weight of its own convolution. Something similar is happening to global financial dynamics today. For three hundred years moneychangers have been making "adjustments" to the seventeenth-century scaffolding of central banking, and now it too is beginning to collapse under the weight of its own convolution. This is what the global economic crisis is really all about, arguments to the contrary notwithstanding.

Money can be said to be the backbone of all structure in economic theory. Beginning with the charter of the Bank of England in 1694, nearly all *new* moneys used by Western civilization as media of exchange have been *borrowed* into general circulation from central banking institutions. This is the reason Western economies don't possess anything resembling a durable backbone. Debt money may prop up the backbone for a while, but eventually it has to be paid back, removing the support for economic structure.

The truth is that in all these years, the same *new* money could have been paid into general circulation free of debt and interest, providing Western civilization with a durable backbone conducive to free enterprise and associated processes of wealth creation. So then why was it that the same *new* money ended up having to be borrowed into general circulation in the form of never ending, self-compounding debt? That is the question.

The rubric of the central banker would answer the question in this way: "New money has had to be borrowed into circulation in order to avoid inflation. If it had been paid into circulation free of debt and interest, politicians would have gone hog wild with the printing presses, and the treasury would have cranked out so much paper that you would have needed a wheelbarrow full of money to buy a loaf of bread."

For three hundred years the rubric and assumption of central banking has read something like this: Unless new money is introduced into circulation in the form of debt, it will eventually lose its value through classic price inflation.

Is the rubric and assumption valid?

Is it consistent with reality?

Since the Federal Reserve Act of 1913 (which in effect legalized the rubric in the United States), most of the *new* moneys that the American people have been obliged to use as media of exchange have been borrowed into general circulation from the nation's central banks (the twelve Federal Reserve banks). Since 1913, the buying power of the US dollar has declined by 95 percent, and the national debt has increased from about $1 billion in 1913 to about $16 trillion at the time of this writing. This suggests the most fundamental assumption of Western economic theory—the rubric and premise of central banking—may be fatally flawed.

You can't fix a broken system on the basis of the same assumption that broke it in the first place—you will bounce off the same walls and end up right back where you started. If you really want to fix a broken system, you must discard the assumption that made it flawed in the first place—the one associated with the seventeenth-century scaffolding of central banking.

Now someone may say, "Well, why can't we just fix the seventeenth-century scaffolding?" Here's the nature of the problem: That rusty, creaky old scaffolding cannot be reformed. It is, by its very nature anti-reform and anti-improvement. It is a debt-creating, debt-compounding system with a built-in "catch 22" that precludes the possibility of reform, for one obvious reason: all of the money and banking courses offered by our institutions of higher learning teach the same three-hundred-year-old *debt system* of money creation. In other words, they teach students of finance how the seventeenth-century scaffolding creates new money *in the form of debt*, the foregone conclusion (the one that escapes all notice) being that this is the *only* way governments can create new money to keep up with economic growth and expansion. Well, that is simply not true. There are other ways of creating *new* purchasing media, as we will discuss later.

From the onset it should be emphasized that the free-enterprise system itself, or the private ownership of property, is not being questioned. God forbid and perish the thought! Indeed, if the American free-enterprise system were allowed to function *freely*, our economy would not be burdened by astronomical debts, horrendous deficits, confiscatory taxation, and *systemic* inflation!

Once again: "We the People" hold our American system of free enterprise in high esteem; we lay great store by it; we equate it with the Protestant work ethic, believing it to be the best scheme devised to promote wealth creation, higher standards of living, and sustained prosperity, progress, and the general felicity of which human civilization is capable. On the other hand, we maintain that the best method of wealth creation will profit no one if the goods and services produced by it end up collecting dust on the shelves because the people do not have access to reliable and durable purchasing media—"good money."

It is the seventeenth-century scaffolding of central banking that we question in this book, not the American free-enterprise system, or the private ownership of property, or the private ownership of the means of production—capitalism. It is the system by which new money is introduced into general circulation that we would now investigate and throw light upon, with a view toward a beneficial change in global economic paradigms.

We Americans have always been an optimistic people. Despite the gloomy prognostications of the doomsayers, we are persuaded that the future looks good. Great things are afoot. Mankind, for centuries held in chains of material want, is about to break free and occupy itself with altogether higher endeavors. In terms of technology, all the ingredients necessary for the making of an advanced civilization on earth are now at hand. The resources are here. The know-how is here. The science is here. The technology is here. The labor is here. The manpower is here. The desire is here. Although some of the spiritual, moral, and ethical elements may still be lacking, all the economic ingredients are here. That is, all but the providence of *good money*.

And how are we to build the new earth without reliable and durable media of exchange? How are we to move toward limitless horizons and transcendent objectives if held down by the shackled quotas of a bizarre economic expedient dating back to the seventeenth century? How are we to meet the quantum needs and unprecedented challenges of the new millennium without first replacing bad money with good money and thereby removing the millstone of soul-consuming debts from the back of nations? That is the question of this eleventh hour.

It is time for the United States of America to answer the question by rising to the occasion and fulfilling her God-given destiny.

The task will not be easy. In principle, the challenge confronting "We the People" today is not too different from the one that confronted America's Founding Fathers in 1776. To say some of the thirteen colonies were apprehensive about cutting the strings that tied them to the providences of King George would be an understatement! The obstacles were indeed great and the consequences of failure dire for the signers of the Declaration of Independence. Had King George and the Tories won the war, America's founders would have been arrested, carted off to England, tried for treason, and hanged.

We thank God for spiritually empowering America's founders to stand their ground, to sever the chains, and usher in a new era of freedom and prosperity on earth. And we see the result of their labor has been productive of good and enduring fruit of every description. For we see here in recorded history the first real and concrete departure from the former ways of corporate ruin and extinction. Not a brief departure, occasioned by happenstance, compulsion, violence, force, mischief, and anarchy; not a chance departure based on wishful thinking, vain philosophy, pious folly, and noble vanity; but a concrete departure, signed, sealed, and ratified in a Constitution and a Bill of Rights affording a legacy of enduring freedom and prosperity for future generations.

Howbeit, these Founding Fathers could not have advanced the providential mandate and destiny of America beyond the reach of their own time and era. Thus the responsibility of advancing that providential mandate and destiny now rests on the shoulders of our generation. It now falls upon We the People to pick up where the Founding Fathers left off and complete the historical undertaking to which they committed their lives and fortunes with a firm reliance on Divine Providence. Naturally this involves three distinct steps, similar to those that founded the nation:

1) Open a rigorous debate in the bicameral chambers of the US Congress, investigating:
    (i) The purpose and role of "money" in human affairs.
    (ii) The deleterious effect of the seventeenth-century scaffolding of central banking on said purpose and role.
    (iii) Alternate, debt-free methods of money creation, with a view toward promoting economic durability, avoiding inflation, and ensuring public accountability.
2) A unanimous Declaration of Independence by all fifty States of the Union from the now-obsolete providences of central banking institutions.
3) The inauguration of a debt-free system of money creation within the framework of an economic Bill of Rights.

In this historic undertaking, We the People and our representatives in Congress would do well to recall the words of Abraham Lincoln, uttered at a pivotal place in the nation's history. This is what Abraham Lincoln said in 1862, with havoc afoot and the Union in jeopardy of dissolution: "The dogmas of the quiet past are inadequate to the stormy present. The occasion is piled high with difficulty, and we must rise with the occasion.

As our case is new, so we must think anew, and act anew. We must disenthrall ourselves, and then we shall save our country."[8]

The occasion is once again piled high with difficulty, and the eyes of the whole world are now turning toward America for leadership. The distinguished members of the United States Congress, supported by the providential wisdom and prayers of We the People must now rise with the occasion and think and act anew. They must disenthrall themselves from the seventeenth-century scaffolding of central banking and save the nation from certain bankruptcy and ruin.

As goes America, so goes the world. The economic fate—the lives and fortunes of multiplied billions created in the image of God in the entire world—hangs in the balance of a historic emancipation such as this.

---

[8] Abraham Lincoln's annual message to Congress, December 1, 1862 (one month before the signing of the Emancipation Proclamation).

Chapter 3

The Foolish Laborer:
Wooden Nickels for Wages

*Men are so simple and yield so readily to the wants of the
moment that he who will trick will always find another
who will suffer to be tricked.*—Niccolo Machiavelli

Once upon a time there lived a poor laborer, an illiterate soul who,
being in want of money, found work on a great farm. On payday he
came to be paid his month's wages. The owner of the farm, a subtle fellow,
knowing the laborer was illiterate, placed a piece of paper in front of him
and told him to sign on the dotted line.

The laborer glanced at the page of fine print before him and, not
willing to admit he was illiterate, asked the owner what he was being asked
to sign. The owner of the farm replied, "Oh, a mere formality."

The laborer hesitated for a moment, but being hard-pressed for the
money signed the document, took the cash, and went home, unaware
that he had just signed a loan contract in the amount he assumed he was
being paid.

A few months later the owner of the farm let it be known that he was
pleased with the laborer, would agree to keep him on, and would increase
his "salary" incrementally if only he would sign a long-term employment
contract. The laborer agreed.

And so it came to pass that the laborer went on working on the
farm, on paydays foolishly signing something he couldn't read on the
dotted line in order to receive the money he needed to keep body and
soul together.

As the seasons and the years went by, however, he began to notice that his "wages" were getting smaller and smaller due to something referred to as "interest deductions." Upon reaching old age he discovered to his horror that he was faced with a colossal debt, and with it the obligation to continue in a state of involuntary servitude with no end in sight.

A strange and sad story, you say? Indeed it is! But could it possibly be a self-portrait of We the People?

The moral of the story should be obvious. One does not reward a laborer by *lending* him the money he has earned, and one does not reward a nation by lending it the money it has earned. Whereas it is the duty of every government to provide the people of its nation with a just, fair, and equitable medium of exchange ("money"), that money should find its way into the arteries of trade and commerce the same way that it should find its way into the pocket of the laborer. If the laborer has earned a hundred dollars, he should be *paid* a hundred dollars, not *loaned* a hundred dollars. As it is *paid outright* to the laborer, so also it should be paid outright to the nation.

When the founders first settled America, they found here a general wilderness. In the span of two hundred years, succeeding generations of Americans have worked hard to convert that wilderness into the most productive civilization on earth, with infrastructures, utilities, superhighways, bridges, irrigation projects, dams, levies, ports, airports, etc. Surely all the public works to that end represent the common labor of We the People. And, surely, a provident and wise legislature could have used those public works as the occasion to pay new moneys into the arteries of industry and commerce free of debt and interest—good money—genuine, sound, durable US dollars backed by the hard work, productive capacity, and providential wealth of the American people.

Financially speaking, America could have been the happiest nation on earth if, in accordance with every sentiment of fairness and equity, the United States Congress had been sober enough to do its constitutional duty by providing the nation with a supply of good money. Instead, that foolish Congress of 1913 "signed on the dotted line," accepting the proverbial loan instead of the outright payment.

It is astonishing and difficult to believe that in all the years in which new money could have been paid into general circulation free of debt and interest, it has instead been borrowed into general circulation in the form of public indebtedness!

Thus, We the People now find ourselves faced with a paradox. The more we progress, the more we owe. The more "affluent" we become, the greater our national poverty! And instead of our growth and our progress making us happier, richer, and better off as a nation, we find ourselves faced with want, scarcity, and a national debt that fastens itself to our ankles like a ball and chain.

Sadder still is that most of our national leaders have been blissfully ignorant of the whole sordid business, obliged like that foolish laborer to sign one "loan contract" after another. Rare are the leaders who were wakeful enough to warn the nation of the consequences of inveterate public indebtedness. We have to go back many years to find even a handful of them.

Certainly Thomas Jefferson issued plenty of warnings to this effect. Part of his letter to a colleague reads thus: "I sincerely believe that banking establishments are more dangerous than standing armies, and that the principle of spending money, to be paid for by posterity, under the name of 'funding,' is but swindling of futurity on a large scale."[9]

Andrew Jackson was another of the nation's leaders who saw the injustice of a debt system of money creation and did not hesitate to cry foul. Jackson was adamant about the nation's wages, and ten thousand wild horses could not have forced him to "sign on the dotted line." This is what he said on the occasion of his veto of the Second Bank of the United States in 1832: "There are no necessary evils in government. Its evils exist only in its abuses. If it would confine itself to equal protection, and as Heaven does its rain, shower its favors alike on the high and the low, the rich and the poor, it would be an unqualified blessing."[10]

Now from the onset it should be emphasized that the bone of contention did not and does not involve the useful and necessary functions that banks perform, and are performing, in our own day and age. The reason Jefferson, Jackson, and a handful of other astute leaders expressed animosity toward

---

[9] Thomas Jefferson, in a letter to John Taylor, Monticello; May 28, 1816.

[10] Andrew Jackson, on the occasion of his veto of the Bank Renewal Bill in 1832. Listed in *The Great Quotations*, compiled by George Seldes (New York: Pocket Books, 1976), 445.

banking institutions was because they saw them as either operating, or having a potential to operate, outside the legitimate bounds of their useful and necessary purviews.

Abraham Lincoln was one president under whose administration the nation's money was paid into general circulation free of debt and interest. The year was 1862, and the president was hard-pressed for money for the civil war. The bullion brokers, seeing they had the president over the barrel, so to speak, said they would loan out no money unless they were paid 28 percent interest for it.

Lincoln refused to submit to such extortion, and turning to the Constitution, directed the Federal Bureau of Engraving to print $450 million in so-called "greenbacks" (called that because of their color). The Congress and the Supreme Court did not challenge his right to do so, nor did Lincoln himself see in the Constitution any limit to his issuing the money directly— without having to pay interest to some middleman.

By January 1863 some $450 million in authentic US dollars were paid into general circulation, free of debt and interest. Those greenbacks stayed in the arteries of the nation's commerce for a hundred years until 1965. Despite their initial depreciation, it has been estimated that in the course of the century or so that they were in circulation, they changed hands enough times to facilitate the exchanges and distributions of goods and services amounting to more than a trillion dollars. What's more, it has been estimated that for the length of time that they were used as good money, they saved the nation and several generations of taxpayers approximately $50 billion in interest payments.

The question might well be asked as to why it was that America was so easily duped and deceived into reverting back to a debt system of money creation/introduction in subsequent years? This question has tried the soul of many an American patriot. Perhaps the answer again lies in the words of Roman orator Marcus Tulius Cicero: "There is no fortress so strong that money cannot take it."[11]

Or, perhaps the fault lies with the profligate generations that stood by with indifference as their public servants did mindlessly "sign on the dotted line." Or perhaps the reason had more to do with the confusion and urgent

---

[11] Marcus Tullius Cicero, *In Verrem*, listed in *The Great Quotations*, compiled by George Seldes (New York: Pocket Books, 1976), 605.

needs of rapid industrialization. Yes, perhaps the real answer has more to do with the magnitude of the changes the nation has been subjected to in such a relatively short period of time. Think of it: for thousands of years mankind knew only the horse and buggy, and then, suddenly and in one generation, mankind took a flying leap from horse and buggy to a manned lunar module on the surface of the moon.

Perhaps it was this welter of change, a maelstrom so intense as to leave little or no time for a moment's reflection, let alone wisdom in monetary matters. The truth is that the need for money has been so great in the last century that We the People, like that foolish laborer, have been content to sign on the dotted line and hurry home with the money, with no time to ask questions about the method of its creation and introduction. But now we of this pivotal generation are suddenly faced with the accumulated burdens of our common folly. And as the nation founders deeper and deeper in debt, truly we can say the chickens have come home to roost.

By now this much should be obvious to all: the three-hundred-year-old debt system of money creation (seventeenth-century scaffolding of central banking) is incongruous with the quantum needs of the new millennium. Without a sea change, there is nothing in store for America and the world but more of the same—more debt, more bad money, more futility, more stagnation, more deficits, more inflation, more taxation, more dependency, more failure, more bankruptcy, more poverty, more penury, and more want and mass misery with no end in sight.

Chapter 4

Money 101 for Dummies:
Back to Basics

All things or services, then, which are to be exchanged must be in some way reducible to a common measure. For this purpose money was invented, and serves as a medium of exchange.—Aristotle

Long ago, "money" did not exist. In those days labor and goods were traded directly without any "buying" and "selling" and this was known as *bartering.*

Bartering was a means of obtaining goods and services needed for living. Despite the undeveloped state of human society, barter was an efficient system—self-tending and self-limiting. No "money management" was required. "Inflation" wasn't possible. No individual could barter with that which he or she did not possess. There was no "currency" to hoard, no "funny money" to speculate with. Junk bonds, derivatives, collateralized-debt obligations (CDOs), mortgage-backed securities (MBOs), credit-default swaps (CDSs)—coffin trades and Wall Street's bet-to-fail shenanigans—did not have ground to exist on.

At first the bartering was of the simple sort, face-to-face and one-on-one—a goat for two pairs of boots, a bushel of wheat for a warm cloak, a gallon of milk for ten iron nails, etc. But as the centuries went by and organized societies began to emerge, bartering was gradually expanded to involve third and fourth parties, until, eventually, it became impossible to keep track of who owed what to whom.

That was the pivotal point in time when "money" was first introduced as a concept.

Focusing on the historical transition point at which bartering was replaced with "buying and selling with money," we see that money was a creation of *expediency*. Money was not an end in itself. It was a means to an end. It became expedient to use money as a means of indirect exchange so that individuals could trade with persons unknown at any time and in any place—as long as they had evidence of prior claims in mutually accepted units of value regarded as "money."

Money was and is *a medium of exchange*. The legitimate and beneficial purpose of money was and is to facilitate the exchanges of goods and services. And since money doesn't grow on trees, we may fast-forward through the centuries and sensibly put forward a rational statement that would go like this: It is the solemn duty of every government to provide a just, fair, and equitable medium of exchange for its citizens—in the form of "money."

In fact it may be stated, as a general and reliable premise, that *a just, fair, and equitable medium of exchange is an essential necessity for the ordering of the affairs of mankind.* More so, and specific to the contemporary function of money, we may sensibly conceive of a related axiom that would read like this: *money is the backbone of all structure in economic theory.*

Just as energy can be said to be the backbone of all structure in physical theory, so also can it be said money is the backbone of all structure in economic theory. If the backbone of the economy is weak, the overall economic structure can be expected to be weak as well. If the backbone is strong, the overall structure can also be expected to be sturdy.

It needs no prophet's eye to see that the overall economic structure of the United States today is weak indeed. How did this happen?

Let us go back to the historical transition when bartering became impractical, and money in various forms was first introduced as media of exchange. Here, the all-important causal relationship that we must fix in our minds can be summed up in a related statement such as the following: came the day when human society passed the stage of simple barter, there arose a need for convenient, mutually agreed-upon media of exchange, a need that was fulfilled in the invention of "money."

We need to dwell on this causal relationship in order to arrive at a sensible and rational understanding of the role of money in human affairs.

Indeed, with all the dogmas, myths, and sophistries by which the concept of money has now been distorted beyond recognition, we need to remind ourselves again and again that money was primarily invented to facilitate the exchanges of goods and services.

Having identified the *primary* purpose of money, we are now in a position to identify its *secondary* purposes. We can say, for example, that money was a creation of expediency intended to provide human society with a basic *unit of account*, a means of effecting transfers of earned credit, a means of establishing the exchange values of labor and goods in relation to one another.

Money was not and is not an end in itself. In, of, and by itself, money has no inherent value. It is *a* unit of account and not physical wealth. It has meaning only when applied to some object, just as the "gallon" has no meaning unless applied to some liquid. No one can trade gallons on Wall Street. No one can buy a gallon or sell a gallon in, of, and by itself. Rather, he or she may buy or sell a gallon of some liquid.

Good Money

Kept within its legitimate role, money can be said to be a blessing. It can be the lifeblood of industry and commerce. It can be purchasing power in the hands of people. It can be a means toward obtaining that sufficiency of nature's goods or real wealth necessary for a meaningful life.

But when money is removed from its legitimate role, when it is stored under a false pretext, when it is sought for itself, or when it is bought and sold as though it were *a commodity*, it can become a curse instead of a blessing.

The falsification of money can give rise to the creation of false values—and false institutions that profit by manipulating those false values. When a government knowingly or unknowingly sanctions the falsification of money, it permits the rise of crooked institutions, not only within its own territorial boundaries, but elsewhere in the world where those institutions have their branches and subsidiaries. When a government allows the falsification of money, that government ends up encouraging unfair financial practices throughout the whole world.

Currency Speculation

Money is a useful instrument as long as it is diligently kept within its intended role as a medium of exchange. When it is removed from that role it vaunts itself on the head of human society, as it is undoubtedly doing today.

Today we may see an array of financial institutions built on the false premise that money is a commodity, to be bought, sold, bargained for, speculated upon, or traded on some "futures market." We may hear on a daily basis about the "trading" going on in the International Monetary Market (IMM) or read about the speculations going on in "currency markets," financial bazaars in which the US *dollar* has perhaps fallen against the European *euro*, or the British *pound* has risen against the Japanese *yen*, or the Russian *ruble* has fallen against the Swiss *franc*, so on and so forth.

How did this happen?

Let us now return to the analogy of the "gallon." It would be absurd to hear about a "gallon market," wouldn't it? If the gallon is a unit of measure, one that determines volumes of liquids to be bought and sold, common sense would require it remain a constant measure. Every sentiment of justice, fairness, and equity would require the gallon (or the liter, as the case may be) to remain a stable denominator of fluids the world over. Yet in the presently convoluted scheme of things, it is as though the gallon has itself become a commodity, to be bought, sold, bargained for, speculated upon, traded, exported, and imported. How did this happen?

Market Fluctuations

We should perhaps digress here to point out that there is nothing wrong or improper about the fluctuations in prices that are caused by the laws of the free market itself. The mischief begins when the "currency factor" compromises and then supersedes the laws of the marketplace.

By way of an analogy, the price fluctuations that may occur by reason of the laws of supply and demand can be likened to the benign ripples on the surface of a lake. These relatively harmless ripples or eddies are natural consequences of free trade and will be found to exist as long as free markets exist.

On the other hand, the across-the-board *national* ups and downs that occur by reason of the fluctuations of global currencies can be likened to man-made tides and tsunamis that can wreak havoc on different nations at different times.

Supply and Demand

All things being equal, the fundamental exchanges of goods and services among nations need be no different (or not too different) from trade and commerce across state boundaries here in the United States. The basic laws that govern supply and demand here in America are no different in the rest of the world. Everything else being equal, the free market will—by the natural restraints of supply and demand—determine the "values" of goods and services in New York and New Delhi alike, allocating fair prices and ratios of exchange, regardless of locality.

A commodity, a resource, a product or service that is scarce will tend to be more costly, hence someone will come along and produce more of it—and its price will stabilize. A commodity that is abundant will tend to be cheap, hence less will be produced—and its price will stabilize.

Free Markets

The assumption that free markets promote prosperous economies is historically reliable. And the idea that prosperous economies can be the harbingers of liberty and guarantors of peace and security is equally reliable. But as long as the currency factor is allowed to compromise the free market—as long as man-made tides and tsunamis are allowed to raise and lower the internal price levels of nations against one another—the hopes and aspirations of mankind for free markets and prosperous economies will remain idle dreams.

One of the greatest injustices that one trading nation could commit against another would be to agree on a price determined by the "value" of a certain currency at the time, letting the people of the other nation depend on that "value" when they take on obligations to import goods, and then allow the "value" of that currency to change so that when payment is due, the purchasers are forced to pay two or three times more than what the original contract called for.

In the presently convoluted scheme of things, we can see how fluctuating currencies—as the ancient bag of deceitful weights—can transform international trade into an occult ritual, if not a cruel and heartless war of attrition in which nations live in perpetual distrust of one another, ever paranoid, ever nervous about the "values" of their currencies.

When a government allows money to be treated in a way in which it should not be treated—*as though it were a commodity*—the same thing can happen to money that happens to other commodities. If more speculators want to sell US dollars than want to buy US dollars, the "worth" will decrease. If more speculators want to buy US dollars than want to sell US dollars, the "worth" will increase.

So how might these ups and downs affect the US economy? Well, to give just one example, if the "cost" of buying US dollars were to rise precipitously against the "cost" of buying European euros, Europeans may find it too "costly" to import US goods! In which case they might cancel or reduce their imports, resulting in proportional declines in the US-based industries and associated tax revenues, proportional increases in US unemployment levels, lowering of the standard of living, so on and so forth.

Just, Fair, and Equitable Systems of Exchange

In the present scheme of things, fair trade is a difficult endeavor. Very often, when transactions have been settled and goods have been shipped, it is discovered too late that currency speculations going on at the time have created a situation in which an obligation of $1,000 can now be fulfilled by the payment of only $900, much to the consternation of the exporting nation. Or, conversely, a situation in which an obligation of $1,000 must now be fulfilled by the payment of $1,100, much to the dismay of the nation importing the goods.

Let us pause to remind ourselves that we are still dealing with the limitations of human nature itself. Given those limitations, it needs no prophet's eye to see that by manipulating currency values, financial traders will be tempted to coordinate investments so commodities are purchased where prices have been artificially lowered and sold where they have been artificially raised. In this way, through coordinating monetary speculation with heavy investments in foreign or domestic securities, bonds, treasuries, gold, industrial shares, and stocks, no doubt many financial institutions are constantly being tempted to try to amass fortunes on the public ruin.

How could this have happened?

Regardless of the how it may or may not have happened, perhaps We the People can agree that the role played by "money" in human affairs is an important one. It cannot be trifled with. It can no longer be swept under a rug. It is a subject that demands the attention of intelligent and thinking people the world over. It is perhaps the most pressing issue confronting We the People and the United States Congress today. Unless addressed, investigated, and its flaws corrected, it may prove to be one of the single greatest obstacles standing in the way of the material relief of the human condition in general.

American Initiative

Nowhere on earth are a people more free to set things right than here in the United States. If We the People cannot straightaway set things right in the whole world, we can at least use the virtues of our American political system to restore money to its legitimate role here in our own God-blessed land. (And just you wait and see if the rest of the world does not follow suit!)

Presently no greater and more solemn duty rests upon We the People and our elected representatives than doing just that.

Chapter 5

Money Creation:
How Do We Introduce New Money into Circulation?

The price we have to pay for money is paid in liberty.
—Robert Louis Stevenson

Insofar as we have ascertained previously that money is *a medium of exchange*, we can also say that unless the supply of money is made to match and balance the volume of trade, exchange will be checked, commerce will be depressed, production will be slowed, and people will be increasingly unable to obtain the goods and services they need.

Now whereas the real wealth of a nation stems in part from the providence of God (agreeable climate, minerals, rich soil, forests, rivers, the bounty of the sea, etc.), and in part from the work ethic, industry, ingenuity, creativity, and productive capacity of its people, the expedient referred to as "money" can only play a subordinate role in facilitating the exchange of the goods and services thus produced. This being the case, the virtue of any *system* of money creation should be evaluated on the basis of the degree in which it contributes to that exchange.

The system that facilitates the exchanges of the greatest volume of goods, services and wealth, should be regarded as the most desirable. And vice versa.

A System of Money Creation

Money is a medium of exchange, and a nation must have a system for creating money. It is precisely this system that we must now discuss, shed light upon, question, and investigate.

When America's founders first settled the continent, they brought little "money" with them. The nation emerged, the states united, and a government was established to secure the union and dispose of civil affairs. The nation was young then, and the amount of money required by the first immigrants was not too great. In the space of two hundred years, however, the North American continent has been transformed into the most productive civilization on earth, with a myriad of small and large companies producing everything from safety pins to wide-bodied jets.

It is easy to see that the amount of money needed to run the nation today is infinitely greater than what it was two hundred years ago—it is easy to see that the *volume of money* has had to be regularly increased in proportion to the growth and expansion of the American economy.

In other words, at regular intervals, new money has had to be *created* and somehow *introduced into general circulation*.

Now the fact that new money has had to be printed is not in itself something we would question or argue about. It is proper for sovereign nations to have the means and the wherewithal to create new money when the need arises. That is not the issue here. But how do you go about introducing the new money into general circulation *after* it has been printed? *That* is the question.

Since the new money itself is a lifeless object knowing no more "good" from "evil" than "right" from "wrong," the bone of contention must therefore surround the *system* by which new money is *introduced* into general circulation after it has been created. More than anything, it is precisely the system of introduction that can give money all of its characteristics, good or bad, and all of its qualities, desirable or undesirable. So we must stop now to ask the question: How on earth do you introduce newly created money into general circulation?

It's certainly not an easy question to answer. It is not as though the Secretary of the Treasury can go up in an airplane, blindfold himself, throw the new money out the window, and hope the prevailing winds will somehow carry it to where it's most needed.

It is again important to emphasize that new money created at the Bureau of Printing and Engraving is not at issue here. What is at issue is the system by which the new money is introduced into the arteries of the nation's commerce, *after* it has been created.

Debt System of Money Introduction

With minor exceptions, the system by which new money is introduced into general circulation in the Western world has been based on debt (seventeenth-century scaffolding of central banking). In this "civilized" world of ours, debt is used as the occasion to introduce new money into general circulation.

How does the debt system work? Imagine newly printed money stacked up in the basement of the US Treasury and ask yourself, "How do we introduce this pile of money into general circulation?" Typically, in a debt system, sovereign nations do not print their own new money or *pay* it into general circulation free of debt and interest. Instead, they may print debt in the form of *bonds* and then use those bonds as the collateral to *borrow* the new money into general circulation from central banks.

To reiterate, typically, within the framework of seventeenth-century scaffolding of central banking, no new paper money can be created and introduced into the arteries of trade and commerce free of debt and interest. The seventeenth-century scaffolding is by its very nature debt-creating and debt-compounding. It exists on a foundation of bonded public indebtedness that can only saddle nations with yokes of *impossible* debt. What is impossible debt?

Desert Island Analogy

A simple analogy may be sought to show what we mean by impossible debt. Imagine, if you will, people permanently stranded on a desert island. They have no money. There are no precious metals on the island. They settle down, establish a makeshift market, and consider inventing a money concept from scratch. But before they can do this, a raft washes up on the beach. On the raft is a central banker who happens to have brought $1,000 with him. The banker discovers the islanders are thinking about devising a system of money creation. He informs them that he already has the money they need. He says they would be far better off just to borrow it from him at a modest 6 percent interest compounded annually.

The islanders form a council, take a vote, and agree. The central banker draws up his loan contract and makes the council sign it. The council takes possession of the $1,000 and in turn contracts with the people. The terms of the contract are simple: the council will use a lottery system to distribute the $1,000 among merchants needing money with which to exchange their goods and services; the merchants will in return issue IOUs to the council in the amount of money they receive. The council will hold on to the IOUs for a period of one year and then use those IOUs to recall (withdraw) the $1,000 from circulation so it can pay back the central banker. The islanders agree.

The new money changes hands in the formative market, and the people use it to "buy" and "sell" what they need. At the end of the year, the council uses the IOUs to recall the $1,000 and pay back the central banker. But now the banker wants an additional $60 in interest, and his loan contract specified that the $60 "must be paid in cash."

The islanders are at a loss. There was no money on the island before the banker arrived, so where is the extra $60 going to come from? The answer is nowhere to be found.

The banker meets with the council and makes another suggestion. He says that since the island is in need of a *system* of money creation, why not let him devise one for them? After all, he is a central banker and that is his specialty, is it not? He says he can easily base the new system on the existing debt—$60—and the council can borrow another $1,000 from him, which the islanders can use as a medium of exchange for another year. He adds that thereafter the islanders won't have to worry about the *principal* on any new loans: they will only have to keep up the *interest* payments on their public debt.

The central banker is persuasive. He suggests the following: if the people will pass a preferential law granting him the exclusive privilege of creating, controlling, and collecting interest on the island's money supply, he in turn will take care of everything and see to it that there is at all times enough money for the islanders to use as a medium of exchange. The council agrees.

As the economy grows and the years go by, the islanders fall deeper and deeper into debt, but the central banker does nevertheless provide enough flow of debt money to keep business going, and on the face of it at least, everything appears to be fine and well.

A generation later, however, the islanders wake up to find that (A) their public debt is ten times greater than all the money in circulation, (B) the price of everything has increased sharply, and (C) the purchasing power of the money they have been using has shrunk precipitously. (The whys and wherefores of A, B, and C will become clear in later chapters.)

Back to Reality

Our oversimplified "desert island" analogy provides useful insight into the nature of a debt system of money introduction. It is easy to see, for example, that it would be impossible for the islanders to borrow their way out of debt. However, in the real world of diversified, industrialized, and interwoven economies, the impossibility of a debt system is well hidden. As long as central bankers are willing to renew or restructure public debts, as long as the ceiling on those public debts can be continually raised, and as long as sufficient "flow" of debt money can be generated to somehow keep businesses going, everything will appear to be fine and well.

But beneath all appearances, beneath the noise and commotion and hubbub of trade and commerce, the sum total liability of the nation will increase and begin to exact from every taxpayer an increasing ransom in life's labor. At a certain stage the compound debt will begin to augment itself exponentially, and that is when the politicians and the people will tear their cloaks, throw dust in the air, wring their hands, and cry, "Alas! Alas! We are undone!"

Since the Federal Reserve Act of 1913, We the People have been laboring under a debt system of money introduction. This is the main reason our national debt is now so huge that it taxes even the imagination! Outwardly we appear to be an affluent nation, but in fact our national wealth can be said to be mortgaged. If all our debts were to be paid, there would not be one red penny left in circulation. In actuarial terms, We the People can be said to be flat broke.

How Did This Happen?

Now, in case some folks are still bewildered and wondering about the excuse given to prop up an irrational scheme of money creation such as this, or the reason given to justify the necessity of issuing the nation's money through a debt system, the excuse and reason would again read something like this: since no one will be able to get the new money too easily without paying interest on it, this will serve to restrain the greedy politicians from printing too much paper money and fostering inflation!

This has been the sort of argument used by central bankers to justify the necessity of a debt system of money creation and introduction. Knowing public opinion is naturally inclined to view politicians with a fair amount of suspicion, central bankers have become skillful at manipulating this straw man. The argument, however, is pure nonsense. While it is true that politicians find themselves wanting to please their constituents by throwing "pork barrel" money at them, and while it is also true that a few of them may be driven by consuming greed and ambition, they are not beyond the reach and control of We the People.

In the first place, politicians do not have the privilege of collecting interest on new money, money that did not exist previously and does not rightfully belong to anyone. In the second place, politicians come and go individually, whereas the central banking institutions that have vested multibillion-dollar interests in the unnecessary creation and increase of global debt are (A) beyond the reach and control of We the People; (B) have been around since the charter of the Bank of England in 1694; and (C) have no intention going away!

In the third place, we are about to show that the *systemic* price inflation that persists in this great country of ours is not caused by too much "printing press money" floating about the place, but is, in fact, an insidious companion of the seventeenth-century scaffolding of central banking itself.

What is a "politician" anyway? This much-maligned denizen of Capital Hill is a public servant elected by We the People, having no authority other than what We the People invest in him or her under the guidelines of the Constitution. What then? What are we to think? Are We the People incapable of disciplining irresponsible and wasteful politicians by way of the voting booth? Assuredly the much-maligned politician is not beyond our accountability or recall.

Central bankers, on the other hand, seem to be immune to any form of public accountability. And if We the People should at any time stir out of our sleep and demand a debt-free system of money creation and introduction, all they have to do is raise the hue and cry of "Printing press money! Printing press money!," and straightaway the Congress and the White House will take fright and go scuttling back to mother.

Consequences of the Existing Debt System

If truth is consistent with reality, then we need not waste our time trying to prove that it is the *existing* debt system that has brought our nation's economy to its knees. *This* is the system under which our nation has been laboring all these decades! *This* is the incumbent system. *This*, and no other system, is responsible for producing most of the mountain of impossible debt now hanging over our own heads and the heads of our children and grandchildren.

Now, again, we do not dispute the fact that spending someone else's money is a favorite pastime of politicians. Indeed, given the flaw in human nature, we probably wouldn't even trust ourselves in their role. But that is precisely why our Founding Fathers incorporated checks and balances into our form of government. With the proper oversight and accountability, We the People *can* create our own money free of debt and interest without destroying its value through inflation.

It *can* be done. To claim it cannot is to insult the integrity and self-governing capacity of We the People. To say it cannot be done is to suggest government *of the people, by the people, and for the people* has perished from the earth.

Chapter 6

Debt-Free System of Money Introduction:
Separation of Bank and State

Congress shall have power to … coin money and regulate the value thereof.—US Constitution, Article 1, Section 8, Paragraph 5

Insofar as individuals have minds, consciences, and wills of their own, we are not here to dictate what they should or should not do with their own finances. If individuals think they can make borrowed money work for them, if they think the dividends they expect to receive on their free enterprise and hard work will exceed the cost of borrowing, that is their own private affair. The bone of contention does not involve the *private* borrowing of money already in existence.

A person who is bound in debt is sometimes called a "bondsman." The individual to whom the person is bound is called a "bondholder." The document that gives the latter a charge over the former is called a "bond." And the association thus created is referred to as "bondage."

An individual may choose to go into debt, which is one thing. Or an individual may be placed in debt by an act of government, which is another thing altogether. In the first instance the debt is incurred privately, with the individual's express foreknowledge and consent. In the second instance it is usually incurred without either.

A debt system of money introduction is based on long-term public indebtedness. It saddles future generations with debts without their consent. It places the debts of one profligate generation on the backs of generations yet unborn, generations that have had no representation and can hardly be expected to pay taxes related to debts they themselves did not incur. We have to remind ourselves that taxation without representation was one of the reasons the American colonies found it necessary to sever the ties that held them to the providences of King George.

We also need to remind ourselves of the words of Thomas Jefferson in a letter that he wrote to James Madison in 1789 when they were discussing limits on contracting debt:

> [T]he earth belongs to each of these generations during its course, fully and in its own right. The second generation receives it clear of the debts and encumbrances of the first, the third of the second, and so on. For if the first [generation] could charge it [the second generation] with a debt, then the earth would belong to the dead and not to the living generation. Then, no generation can contract debts greater than may be paid during the course of its own existence.[12]

When a living generation is placed in debt by a previous (dead) generation, the living generation must work to earn money with which to pay taxes, with which to service the debts of the dead generation. The term that we would apply to this business is indeed "bondage."

The national debt of the United States has now climbed to more than $16 trillion. Unborn generations are now hopelessly in debt, thanks to the common folly of our generation. How will those future generations, our children and grandchildren, regard us? How will they judge us? What will they have to say about us? They will no doubt say this: "We have to work and sweat to earn the bread that the dead have eaten!"

The Function and Responsibility of Government

We previously ascertained that a just, fair, and equitable medium of exchange is an essential necessity for ordering the affairs of mankind. Since the government of the United States was instituted to do just that (secure the union, maintain the peace, dispose of civil and national affairs—order the

---

[12] Thomas Jefferson, to James Madison, September 6, 1789. Listed in *The Writings of Thomas Jefferson*, Memorial Edition, Lipscomb and Bergh, editors (Washington, DC, 1903–04), 7:455.

affairs of the nation), it follows that one of its most solemn responsibilities has to do with the provision of "money."

In this connection we would now submit the following dichotomy, with a view toward making a clear separation between the responsibilities of the federal government and the responsibilities of the private banks. A separation has to be made between the following:

1) The *creation/introduction* of new money by the federal government.
2) The safekeeping and lending of that money by the banks.

The point to be made here is that when referring to the creation of new money, it must be understood that the function is exclusively reserved to the federal government under Article 1, Section 8, Paragraph 5 of the US Constitution. On the other hand, safekeeping and lending *existing moneys* is the function commonly associated with private banks.

Despite the fact that these two functions would nowadays seem to be convoluted, in principle they are entirely separate.

The Federal Reserve System

An oversimplified theory of the Federal Reserve System might go something like this: In order for the US Congress to be able to create the nation's money (A) without conflict of interest and (B) without destroying its value by "politicians printing too much paper money," the Congress would have to appoint a sort of a blind trust, a non-political, non-partisan mediator—the Federal Reserve (or the "Fed," as it is called).

The Fed would then assess the needs of the economy and regulate the creation of new money as necessary. The new money would be introduced into general circulation through the portals of the commercial banks. The people would borrow the new money into general circulation from the commercial banks, use it to buy what they need, run their businesses, pay their workers, etc. And so, the new money would change hands and diffuse naturally into the arteries of the economy.

On the face of it, the above scenario sounds plausible. Regrettably, the Federal Reserve and other central banks around the world were all structured around the seventeenth-century scaffolding that is now collapsing under the weight of its own convolution.

Debt-Free System of Money Introduction

Under the guidelines of an alternative, new, but fully constitutional debt-free system, the responsibility of money creation and introduction would rest with the US Congress itself, possibly mediated through an impartial institution, a non-political, non-partisan blind trust. Something like the present Fed, only completely restructured into a subordinate and transparent arm of the US Congress itself—a "New Fed."

How would a debt-free method of money creation work? Well, the system would be new, unfamiliar, and initially awkward, but in principle quite sound and workable.

Example: State governments would submit their monetary needs along with standardized case studies, reviews, evaluations, assessments, impact reports, costs, bids, timelines, benchmarks, projections, etc. to the Congress. The New Fed arm of Congress would review these and come back with its recommendations. Upon approval, and in full compliance with Article 1, Section 8, Paragraph 5 of the US Constitution, the Congress would authorize the New Fed to create the new money and *pay* it into general circulation free of debt and interest through the portals of the twelve New Fed Reserve Banks, bypassing the commercial banks.

For example, the New Fed Bank in Dallas would work with the Texas Secretary of the Treasury (and by extension, state and local governments in Texas) to *pay* contractors with lowest bids to build or repair Texas highways, transit systems, local roads, bridges, dams, levies, waterways, airports, seaports, public buildings, parks, recreation areas, utilities, transmission lines, and other projects that may fall under the category of "Texas Public Works."

Similarly, the New Fed Bank in Chicago would work with the Illinois Secretary of the Treasury (and by extension, state and local governments in Illinois), to *pay* public works contractors in Illinois. The New Fed Bank in Atlanta would work with the Georgia Secretary of the Treasury (and by extension, state and local governments in Georgia), to *pay* public works contractors in Georgia. The New Fed Bank in San Francisco would work with the California Secretary of the Treasury (and by extension, state and local governments in California), to *pay* public works contractors in California, and so on and so forth.

The numerous contractors would then use the new moneys to buy what they need, pay their workers, etc., whereupon the new moneys would diffuse naturally into general circulation, the surpluses thereof accumulating in individual and corporate savings accounts at the private banks.

The private banks would then be securely positioned to lend some of those surpluses to the private sector at competitive rates. Creative entrepreneurs and enterprising corporations could avail themselves of that surplus credit, borrowing it from the private banks at competitive rates, and using it to build the nation at the level of the grassroots, the incentive being toward healthy competition, creativity, innovation, ingenuity, efficiency, productivity, and hard work.

In this way, within the framework of a debt-free system of money creation and introduction, most of the financial obligations incurred by We the People would fall under the category of "private debt," with little if any "public debt" to speak of to encumber future generations. There may well be failures in the private sector. Sloppy business ventures and inefficient corporations may—by the grace of Almighty God—go bankrupt, but the fiscal integrity of the nation as a whole will remain intact and government of the people, by the people, and for the people will never be in default.

Granted that the example we have provided here is an oversimplification of how a debt-free system of money creation and introduction might work. Granted also, that later in this publication we will suggest an even more holistic and streamlined system. For now, however, let us stand our ground and not be swayed by the doomsday counsels of those central bankers who would have us believe that *paying* new money into general circulation *free of debt and interest* would amount to the blackest and most damnable sin that any sovereign government could commit in the universe.

Of All Sad Words of Pen and Tongue

The Federal Reserve System, with its twelve strategically and conveniently located Federal Reserve Banks, might have been the means toward such a felicitous scenario (in the immortal words of John Greenleaf Whittier: "Of all sad words of pen or tongue, the saddest are these: 'It might have been'!"). The Fed might have been that blind trust, that non-partisan, non-political mediator responsible for the creation, introduction, and regulation of the nation's basic money supply. The Fed might have been the catalyst in an otherwise self-limiting, self-stabilizing economy with control, management, interference, and taxation kept to a minimum.

Most regrettably, however, the Fed has been rendered the practitioner and purveyor of the three-hundred-year-old debt system! Be it because of the lackadaisical Congress of 1913 that ratified the Federal Reserve Act (during a Christmas recess, of all things), or be it because of improvident legislation subsequently signed into law, or be it because of public ignorance and a general listlessness on the part of We the People, the Fed has been allowed to supersede the constitutional role of sovereign government in the creation and introduction of new money.

We could have had a debt-free system of money creation and introduction in America, and with it the most productive and stable economic disposition of any nation on earth—a generally debt-free beacon of economic liberty for the whole world to emulate. Sad to say, we have had the exact opposite—booms, busts, crashes, depressions, recessions, failures, unemployment, inflation, deficits, and a national debt that hangs over the heads of our children, and our children's children, like a plague.

There *are* no necessary evils in government! There *is* no law that compels a nation—on pain of hellfire and damnation—to introduce its own newly created money into general circulation by way of the seventeenth-century scaffolding of central banking. The three-hundred-year-old debt system has outlived its usefulness. It is fatally flawed and needs to be replaced by debt-free methods of money creation/introduction throughout the whole world.

An Issue of Sovereignty

Common sense alone would indicate that the people of a sovereign nation ought not be dependent on privately owned central banking institutions for the creation of their own media of exchange. It is the constitutional duty and responsibility of duly elected and representative government to provide a just, fair, and equitable medium of exchange for its people, and not the duty, responsibility—or prerogative—of private banks to do so.

The Founding Fathers of America were quite clear about this: Congress shall have power to … coin money and regulate the value thereof … (US Constitution, Article 1, Section 8, Paragraph 5).

Chapter 7

Debt System versus Debt-Free System:
Debt Money versus Debt-Free Money

Money is the lifeblood of the economy, and unless it
circulates readily, the essential economic activities go into
the equivalent of cardiac arrest.—Gillian Tett[13]

Insofar as we have ascertained that money is *a medium of exchange*, we may also refer to it as "the lifeblood of trade and commerce."

When there is a hemorrhage, the vital signs of the human body will begin to fluctuate. If the hemorrhaging continues, the body will eventually go into shock. So also when the money supply (the lifeblood of trade and commerce) begins to hemorrhage, the vital signs of the economy will begin to fluctuate. If the hemorrhaging continues, the economy will go into the equivalent of cardiac arrest—the shock of a depression.

New money introduced into circulation via a debt-free system would enter the arteries of trade and commerce and stay there more or less indefinitely (no hemorrhage). Contrariwise, when governments introduce new money into circulation through the debt system associated with the seventeenth-century scaffolding of central banking, the money cannot stay in the arteries of trade and commerce. Why? Because at a later date it has to be retired, withdrawn, taxed, and bled-off to pay or to service the public debt (hemorrhage).

In the context of the proposed debt-free system, the new money would be *paid* into general circulation and rendered a more or less permanent

---

[13] Gillian Tett, *Fool's Gold* (New York: Simon and Schuster, Inc., 2009), 25.

medium of exchange. Contrariwise in the existing debt system, the same new money has to be *borrowed* into circulation, and in principle at least, We the People will have no permanent medium of exchange to rely on. Instead we will have to rely on the ongoing "flow" of debt money, parts of which must be continually bled-off to service the public debt. And unless the blood that is lost is replaced by ongoing transfusions of new debt money (more borrowing), the economy may slide into throes of a recession or depression.

Granted, we are oversimplifying the differences between the existing debt system of new money introduction, and our proposed debt-free system of money introduction. Granted also that some money—even debt money—is better than no money. But let us not fall into the error of confusing the two systems. The existing debt system and our proposed debt-free system are as different as darkness and light.

The Limitations of Human Nature

Something else has to be considered here as well. Let us remind ourselves that we are yet dealing with the limitations of human nature itself! Given those limitations, it is easy to see that if money is made scarce, it will tend to increase the power of those who create and control it. To quote Woodrow Wilson:

> A great industrial nation is controlled by its system of credit. Our system of credit is concentrated. The growth of the nation therefore and all our activities are in the hands of a few men, who even if their actions be honest and intended for the public good, are necessarily concentrated upon the great undertaking in which their own money is involved, and who, necessarily, by every reason of their own limitations, chill and check and destroy genuine economic freedom.[14]

---

[14] President Woodrow Wilson: 1911; quoted by US Supreme Court Justice Louis Brandeis in his collection of essays, *Other People's Money and How Banks Use Them,* published in 1914. Listed in *The Great Quotations,* compiled by George Seldes (New York: Pocket Books, 1976), 241.

Where there is plenty, nothing can be held in ransom. But where there is chronic scarcity, the natural and inexorable progress of things will be toward monopoly, control, concentration, and centralization of power. Given the limitations associated with human nature, the sad truth is that "power corrupts, and absolute power corrupts absolutely."[15] If the theory of the government of the United States is opposed to the unlimited deposit of power in one place, it is precisely because America's founders were familiar with this sad truth.

Given the foibles associated with human nature, it seems obvious that by the very nature of things—by natural progress—there is a high probability that the volume of money in general circulation will be less than what is needed, ergo scarcity in various disguises will tend to become a rule of thumb in a debt system. And since money is the medium that We the People need to exchange our goods and services with, it also seems obvious that periods of economic prosperity will nearly always be followed by periods of economic privation.

The very nature of a debt system, coupled with the limits of human nature itself, makes long-term economic stability well-nigh unobtainable. In the short run, things may go well now and then as the flow of debt money swells with new transfusions of borrowing. In the long run, however, there will be major ups and downs, major disruptions in the economy coupled with inveterate scarcity. Be it by reason of "hemorrhage" or by reason of the shortcomings of human nature itself, an economy that is built on a foundation of debt is one built on sand.

The national debt of the United States is presently in excess of $16 trillion. As to the rate of the "interest hemorrhaging" now in effect, and the magnitude of the overall losses in terms of trade, commerce, confidence, jobs, tax revenues, and general prosperity, we can only leave those to the imagination of the reader.

Cause and Effect

Our economy is not failing due to inexplicable reasons. Debt, poverty, privation, unemployment, chronic inflation, and associated failures do not

---

[15] The most likely source of this saying is in a letter written by the English historian and moralist Lord Acton (1834–1902) to Bishop Creighton in 1887.

suddenly rear their ugly heads in the most affluent nation on earth without cause. Since the Federal Reserve Act of 1913 America has been laboring under a debt system of money creation, obliged to borrow herself into oblivion and endure all the consequences of that error in cyclic recessions, booms, busts, depressions, panics, crashes, failures, meltdowns, mass foreclosures, and bankruptcies, to say nothing of breadlines and soup kitchens.

The deficits that go hand in hand with the whole sordid business are now in the process of snowballing exponentially. The disturbing trends, facts, figures, and statistics before us will not reverse themselves without a sea change in our method of money creation and introduction. They will continue to snowball out of control until We the People come to our senses, get off the couch, and replace the obsolete debt system with a debt-free system. No generation has ever faced a financial burden such as this, and never has it been more necessary for a people to right themselves with respect to the whole question of "money" than for We the People.

The economic disaster now confronting the United States can be likened to that of a ship that is sinking at sea, a ship with a breach to its hull. At first the water begins to leak in slowly, not too much to worry about. As long as some of the water can be pumped out, the ship can be kept afloat for a while longer. But soon, a sort of creeping paralysis sets in. As the deficit between the water pouring in and the water being pumped out widens, there is a point of no return beyond which the process becomes irreversible. The greater the deficit, the greater the dead weight of the ship. The greater the dead weight of the ship, the greater the rate at which the sea will flood her holds. Suddenly the process achieves critical mass. The proud ship lists, rolls, and sinks in a matter of minutes.

"Printing-Press Money! Printing-Press Money!"

There *are* no necessary evils in government. Yet generations of Americans and their legislators have been conditioned into believing a national debt is a necessary evil. To hear central bankers talk you would think We the People were absolutely incapable of creating our own debt-free medium of exchange without destroying its value through inflation. Rare is the senator or congressman who has ever dared even suggest the possibility of creating the nation's money via a debt-free system. Why? Because at the very mention of such a possibility, central bankers will become hysterical, launch into their tirades, and issue dire warnings about "printing-press money," reminding us of the calamities that have occurred when nations have attempted to issue their own money free of debt and interest.

The central banking institutions that create and control global debt have in the course of their extensive and accumulative experiences developed a keen sense of their own advantage with respect to the power of granting or withholding credit to or from sovereign nations. They know, by instinct if by nothing else, that the way to preserve the safety and longevity of their institutions lies in instilling among the general public a religious horror of "printing-press money!" It has been their *policy* to infuse into the minds of the public an attitude that regards the "printing" of money with a jaundiced eye, even viewing it as one of the blackest, most damnable and unpardonable sins of the body politic.

Americans have been conditioned about the so-called "evils" of paper money to such an extent that it is not uncommon to find even the most sensible of our senior citizens throwing disdainful glances at Washington and making statements such as, "Yes, well, the politicians just go down to the basement and print more money!"

The mainstream media have also been conditioned to this effect, and it is not uncommon to find editorials in financial columns warning about "the evils of paper money," or opinions to the effect that "the government is fueling inflation by virtue of its uninhibited production of printing-press money!"

We would have the American people, and people around the world, be aware of the central banker's infamous boogeyman: "Printing-press money! Printing-press money!"

Question: If politicians could just "go down to the basement and print more money," how in heaven's name could the government be in debt to begin with? (Try answering that question!)

If Uncle Sam could just go down in the basement and "print money," why would he be gnawing at the taxpayers' bones and scratching the rude prairie earth in the hope of finding fresh sources of revenue? Why doesn't he just "print" the money and pay off his debts? Answer: Because he is terrified of the central banker's scarecrow: "Printing-press money!"

The moment the suggestion is made that We the People have a constitutional right to issue our own media of exchange free of debt and interest, up goes the central banker's cry of alarm: "Printing-press money! Printing-press money!"

Central bankers are keenly aware of the power that this scarecrow wields over the guilty consciences of politicians, so it is not surprising to find them using subtle anecdotes, such as "throwing paper money out of airplanes" or "taking a wheel-barrow full of paper money to the supermarket to buy a loaf of bread." Indeed, they are fond of reminding us of the disasters that followed on the heels of the severe price inflation that occurred in Germany in 1923. What they conveniently avoid mentioning, however, is that the German leaders of that time used inflation as a ploy and a strategy to get rid of their war debt.

"Wheelbarrow Full of Paper Money!"

When Germany fell in 1918, the Allies met in the mirrored halls of the Palace of Versailles to decide the terms of peace. In the Treaty of Versailles, it was decided that Germany would have to pay a reparation bill of $132 billion in gold or pre-war marks (a truly staggering sum in those days).

A few years later, as it turned out, the German leaders used inflation as a means of ridding themselves of the Versailles debt. Inflation was used as a deliberate ploy, a stratagem, a gambit. The German printing presses were kept going around the clock, and the money supply was increased at a rate bordering on the absurd until a thousand marks—which prior to 1923 would have bought about 250 US dollars—could barely buy a loaf of bread.

Perhaps we should also point out that the severe inflation that seized hold of Russia subsequent to the October Revolution in 1917 was similarly carried out as a matter of deliberate policy—the Bolsheviks destroyed the purchasing power of the ruble in an effort to drive out the last vestiges of capitalism in Russia.

The central banker's scarecrow notwithstanding, the fact remains that prudent increases in the nation's money supply have nearly always proved beneficial. Conversely, every instance in which the nation's supply of money has been curtailed has resulted in stagnation and misery. This, again, is because money is the lifeblood of industry and commerce! Money is purchasing power in the hands of We the People. Money makes possible the exchanges of goods and services. Money greases the wheels that *produce* those goods and services, creating the jobs and the national wealth that gives strength to the economy.

Now, it is not being suggested the government printing presses be set loose to litter the streets of America with hundred-dollar bills, or for the Fed Chairman to start "throwing paper money out of airplanes" (as our friends at the Fed, at the World Bank, at the International Monetary Fund and at the London School of Economics will no doubt be accusing us of doing). And neither should Uncle Sam resume borrowing himself into bankruptcy.

The suggestion is that our elected representatives in Washington should familiarize themselves with the fundamental difference between the fickle medium of exchange that has to be introduced into general circulation via a debt system dating back to the seventeenth century, and the more permanent and reliable medium of exchange that can now be introduced into general circulation via a debt-free system. Above all, our elected representatives should stand their ground and stop bolting to the stampede at the first cry of "printing-press money!"

There is no such law that says, "New money has to be borrowed into circulation; otherwise it will end up being worthless." There is no such axiom, no such rule of logic and divination. No nation has to *borrow* its own media of exchange into circulation from central bankers.

The very concept of money is based on shared faith and mutual trust. Our English word "credit" is itself derived from the Latin *credo, credere*, "to entrust, lend; have confidence in; to believe."[16]

If a nation can find within itself the trust, confidence, power, and authority to issue a *dollar bond* via a debt system dating back to the seventeenth century, it can find within itself the trust, confidence, power, and authority to issue a dollar bill via a debt-free system in the twenty-first century. The same trust, confidence, power, and authority (fiat) that made the *bond* "good" will make the *bill* "good" as well.

---

[16] *Collins Gem Latin Dictionary* (New York: HarperCollins, 1999), 88.

Chapter 8

Classic Price Inflation:
Too Much Money, Chasing Too
Few Goods and Services

*Ordinary tyranny, oppression, excessive taxation, these bear lightly on
the happiness of the mass of the community, compared with fraudulent
currencies and robberies committed by depreciated paper.*—Daniel Webster

Insofar as money itself is a lifeless object, knowing no more good from bad
than right from wrong, it must be the system by which money is *introduced*
into circulation that gives it its desirable or undesirable characteristics.

Inflation seems to have plagued almost every civilization on earth. It
is an insidious menace that creeps up on societies and disembowels them
without a single shot being fired. In many respects it is more dangerous
than the visible foe with its armies, tanks, battleships, and warheads.

Circa 300 AD, during the reign of the emperor Diocletian, the price
inflation was so severe that it is thought to have contributed to the downfall
of the Roman Empire. The severe inflation that seized hold of Germany in
1923 is thought to have paved the way for the rise of Hitler. In China, it is
thought to have been the prelude to the mass upheavals that set the stage
for the rise of Mao Zedong.

Today in America we have this thing called "inflation," and despite
the fact that it has a historic reputation for devouring societies from
within, no one in authority seems to understand the real causes of it. The
traditional "cures" are not working in this case. The Federal Reserve policy
of "tightening credit" is not bringing the *underlying* rate of inflation under
control.

The Consumer Price Index (CPI)[17] is a statistical tool the government uses to gauge the rate of inflation in America, and the "base period" is a year that the government arbitrarily chooses as a starting point to do that. Despite the fact that in computing the CPI the government has been repeatedly advancing base periods(!), the fact remains the domestic purchasing power of the dollar has dwindled from one hundred cents in 1913 to less than five cents today. The picture that comes to mind is that of a swimmer caught in the grip of an outgoing riptide. He seems to be swimming toward the shore, but in actuality the undercurrent is taking him out to sea.

Correct Diagnosis

When a physician is confronted with a disease, the first thing he must do is correctly diagnose it. Many diseases have overlapping symptoms, and some diseases, although very different, have similar symptoms. For example, if the symptoms include persistent skin disorders, they may be caused by a simple allergy or irritation or may be caused by cancer. The correct diagnosis is, therefore, an important part of the overall cure. If the physician is skilled in his art, he will first determine the cause of his patient's skin disorders. Only after he has done this will he begin a course of treatment.

Needless to say, we are equating inflation with an economic disease, and we are saying that correct diagnosis is the first step toward an eventual cure.

Classic Price Inflation

The best way to understand what economists may refer to as *classic price inflation* would be to think of the free market as a gigantic auction hall. So let us now simplify everything and imagine that we are in an auction

---

[17] The CPI (Consumer Price Index) in the United States is defined by the Bureau of Labor Statistics as "a measure of the average change over time in the prices paid by urban consumers for a market basket of consumer goods and services," base periods being starting points for measuring the change. Their website also has a handy inflation calculator: http://www.bls.gov/data/inflation_calculator.htm.

hall, with sellers at their booths, buyers roaming around, and auctioneers doing their job by trying to bid up prices. The most important thing to bear in mind in this auction hall is *there are no fixed prices here*!

In this auction hall, sellers will try to get the highest prices for their goods, and buyers will try to pay as low a price as they can. If a seller is asking too much, the buyer can go buy what he wants from another seller. If a buyer is offering too low a bid, the seller can sell his wares to another buyer.

Effective Demand

In this auction hall, *effective demand* will largely determine the highest prices that sellers will be able to get for their products. But what are we to understand by effective demand? Well, for one thing, we are to understand a *desire* on the part of buyers to get their hands on a product or item—if they want it badly enough they may be willing to pay a higher price for it. More importantly, however, effective demand relates itself to the amount of money that buyers have in their pockets. That is, the volume of money floating about in the auction hall.

If the level of effective demand is high, the auctioneers will succeed in bidding up prices. If the level of effective demand is low, the auctioneers will have to settle for lower prices.

One Violin for Sale

Let us imagine the auctioneer is trying to sell a violin to interested buyers, and let us imagine it is the only violin in the entire auction hall. Question: At what "price" will the bidding start, and at what "price" will it end? Well, if buyers have on average about $10 in their individual pockets, it is reasonable to assume the bidding may begin at around $3–4 and end at about $9–10.

But suppose the buyers in the auction hall have on average about $100 in their pockets, what then? At what "price" would the bidding start and at what "price" would it end? Well, it would be reasonable to assume that bidding might begin at around $30–40 and end at about $90–100.

And if the buyers in the auction hall have on average about $1,000 in their pockets, at what "price" would the bidding start, and at what "price" would it end? Well, again, it would be reasonable to assume that the bidding might begin at around $300–400 and end at about $900–1000.

And if the buyers in the auction hall had on average about $1 million in their pockets? (You get the picture.)

Here is the point: Not only are there no fixed prices in the auction hall, but the prices that come and go in it are to a great extent dependent on the *volume of money in general circulation*.

This is, of course, an oversimplified analogy, equating the free market with an auction hall and limiting what is being called "volume of money" to the aggregate of what the buyers in that auction hall may have in their pockets. Nevertheless, the conclusion to be drawn here, one of the basic premises of classical economics is as follows: the greater the volume of the money floating about in the auction hall, the higher the general "prices." The smaller the volume of money floating about in the auction hall, the lower the general "prices."

We don't need a degree from the London School of Economics to see that "prices" will tend to level themselves against the volume of money floating about in the auction hall. And we don't need to be lectured by the chairman of the Federal Reserve to understand why government must keep a watchful eye on the volume of money floating about in the proverbial auction hall, precisely because "prices" will tend to level themselves against it. The moral is simple: the volume of money in the auction hall must be increased prudently and in proportion to increases in the volume of goods/ services being brought to market in it.

Question: What would happen if the volume of money were to be increased too rapidly, out of all proportion with the volume of goods/ services being brought to market?

Answer: it would result in a temporary *imbalance* between the volume of money and the volume of goods/services, in which case the auctioneers would succeed in bidding up prices—classic price inflation.

The reverse would hold true also. What would happen if the volume of money were to be suddenly decreased in proportion to the volume of goods/services? Answer: the auctioneers would have to settle for lower prices—classic price deflation.

Industrial Maturity

In light of the above, and given a broader perspective, it is logical to assume that classic price inflation can be caused by *industrial immaturity* as well. What does *industrial immaturity* mean? It is the incapacity of a nation to offset and balance rapid increases in the volume of money with rapid increases in volumes of goods/services.

Let's return to our violin analogy. The reason the auctioneer was able to bid up the price of the violin so high was because it was the only violin for sale in the entire auction hall. However, if ten or a hundred or more similar violins were to be quickly brought to market, the "price" of each would fall exponentially.

The conclusion to be drawn here, loosely referred to as "supply-side economics" or sometimes "Reaganomics" (providing an incentive for increased production by reducing taxes and government interference), may read as follows: if the obstacles to production could be removed, the volume of goods and services in the auction hall would be able to rapidly increase to keep up with increases in the volume of money floating about in it, and in this way classic price inflation could be generally avoided.

To reiterate: Classic price inflation is caused by an *imbalance* between two things: the volume of money floating about in the auction hall, and the volume of goods and services in it. If these two things could be kept balanced, there would be no classic price inflation to speak of.

It can be seen, therefore, that industrial maturity has a bearing upon the occurrence of classic price inflation. If a nation is industrialized to the point where it can quickly increase the production of goods and services, then no reasonable increases in the volume of money floating about in the auction hall could lead to classic price inflation. Why not? Because the economy would go into high gear and rapidly crank up additional goods and services to match, balance, offset, and equalize the increases in the money supply.

Lesser Developed Nations

In light of the above, we could argue that classic price inflation would tend to be indigenous to the lesser-developed nations of the world. The inflation that was rampant in the petroleum exporting (OPEC) nations a few decades ago was, for the most part, classic price inflation. It was caused by an *imbalance* between the volumes of oil money flooding into the auction halls of those nations and the volumes of goods and services being offered in them.

Huge revenues from the sale of oil poured into the auction halls of the OPEC nations. Suddenly, buyers found a great deal of money in their pockets with relatively little to spend it on, and the "auctioneers" succeeded in bidding up the prices of the few goods that were available for sale. In other words, those lesser-developed nations did not at that time have the industrial maturity to match, balance, equalize, and offset the glut of oil money with the rapid production of new goods and services. A temporary imbalance ensued between volume of money and volume of goods/services. This imbalance caused general prices to float upward.

And this is how economists derive their own understanding of classic price inflation (using their own jargon): "Too much money, chasing too few goods and services."

Too Much Money, Chasing Too Few Goods and Service

When contemporary economists speak about "inflation," they are—to a man—referring to classic price inflation. In other words, they all believe the inflation that has eroded the buying power of the dollar in the last ninety years has been caused by "too much money, chasing too few goods and services." This was, and to a great extent remains the rationale behind the Federal Reserve's policy of trying to "cure" inflation by tightening credit (reducing the volume of money in the auction hall).

A typical "cure" scenario would go something like this: The CPI (Consumer Price Index) tells the Fed that general prices are rising too quickly. The Fed, believing that rising prices are caused by too much money, chasing too few goods and services, raises the basic interest rates, shrinking the volume of money floating about in the proverbial auction hall. With less money floating about in the auction hall, the auctioneers settle for lower prices, and the Fed can claim it is keeping inflation under control.

Now we do not deny that classic price inflation is to be avoided at all costs. Classic price inflation is detrimental to society because, among other things, inordinate increases in the nation's money supply do not filter down into all pockets equally, resulting in injustice with respect to those who are on fixed incomes, or no income, for example. Classic price inflation is also bound to be injurious to world trade because of the way in which it can raise and lower the internal price levels of trading nations against each other, compromising fair trade.

Curing Classic Price Inflation

Yes, yes, by all means, classic price inflation must be guarded against by all governments whose duty it is to provide their people with just, fair, and equitable media of exchange. Fortunately, however, classic price inflation is not too difficult to diagnose or cure. Why? Because the imbalances that bring it about are neither complex nor mysterious.

Classic price inflation is the result of a relatively simple and straightforward causal relationship. It is caused by an imbalance between the volume of money floating about in the proverbial auction hall, and the volume of goods and services being traded in it. With classic price inflation, the increases in general prices are neither arcane nor difficult to explain. Rather each successive increase in the volume of money—each successive plateau—can be seen to correspond with a proportional rise in general prices (and vice versa).

Classic price inflation can be brought under control by timely governmental intervention. For instance, if a government ascertains that the volume of money floating about in the auction hall has increased out of all proportion with the volume of goods and services being traded in it, government would be justified to take the excess money out of circulation by various legal means at its disposal. One such means would be to raise interest rates, per standard Federal Reserve policy. A more draconian way would be for the government to impose a temporary luxury tax, by so doing rapidly taking the excess out of circulation while sparing the poor and needy.

A far better and more holistic way, however, would be for the government to institute measures that would unshackle production, streamline industry and encourage the rapid production of "more violins," per the late President Reagan's understanding of the "supply-side" dynamic.

If the "inflation" that has been eroding the buying power of the US dollar in the last ninety years had been of the classic variety ("too much money, chasing too few goods and services"), then we could have reasonably assumed that the Federal Reserve policy of "tightening credit" would have stood a good chance of curing it. Regrettably, and as we are about to show, the chronic inflation that is gnawing away the substance of the American economy is caused by something altogether different.

Chapter 9

Systemic Price Inflation:
Too Little Money, Chasing Too Much Debt

*Consider how you have fared. You have sown much, but harvested little;
you eat, but you never have enough; you drink, but you never have your
fill; you clothe yourselves, but no one is warm; and you that earn wages
earn wages to put them into a bag with holes.*—Haggai 1:5–6 (RSV).

In ancient history there is a story about a court official who performed
a notable service for King Shirham of India. The king, not wishing to
remain in the official's debt, said he would grant him any reasonable reward
he chose. The official, a clever individual, placed a chessboard before the
king, put a grain of wheat on the first square, and said, "If it please my
lord the king to double the grain of wheat according to the number of the
squares on the chessboard, I will take the sum and go."

The king, overjoyed to be rid of the official so easily, agreed to grant
him the boon. His servants brought wheat, placed one grain on the first
square of the chessboard, two grains on the second, four grains on the next,
eight on the next, sixteen on the next, thirty-two on the next, sixty-four
on the next, and so on. At first the increases were small, hardly anything
to worry about. But as the process began to snowball, it wasn't long before
the proud king discovered to his horror that there would not be enough
wheat in his entire kingdom to pay the official.

The Nature of Compound Debt

By way of a grand introduction to the subject of *systemic price inflation*, we would have readers glance at the following table, familiarize themselves with the character of compound debt, and take note of the alarming way in which it will balloon if the principal is left untouched over the decades.

$1,000 Borrowed into Circulation at 6 Percent Compound Interest per Year

Debt	Years	Amount Due
$1,000	12	$2,012
"	24	$4,049
"	36	$8,147
"	48	$16,394
"	60	$32,988
"	72	$66,378
"	84	$133,565
"	96	$268,755
"	108	$540,796
"	120	$1,088,188

From this table it can be seen that if both principal and interest are left unpaid on a $1,000 debt for twelve years, it will take about twice as much money (an additional $1,012) to pay it off. What will the merchants in our proverbial auction hall have to do in order to come up with the additional $1,012?

Look at the table and fetch your calculator. If the same debt is left unpaid for forty-eight years, it will take about sixteen times as much money to pay it off. What will our merchants have to do to come up with the additional $15,394?

If left unpaid for 120 years, it will take more than 1,000 times as much money to pay it off. What will merchants have to do to come up with the additional $1,087,188?

The answer in all cases is this: *they would certainly have to raise their prices!*

Granted, we are assuming our auction hall is a closed system; and, here again, we are oversimplifying what's going on in it. However, given that our actual American debt system has been in effect since the Federal Reserve Act of 1913, and given that the principal on our national debt has been left more or less unpaid in all these years, this suggests that the 95 percent decline in the purchasing power of the dollar since 1913 may in fact be endemic to the Federal Reserve System itself.

Back to the Auction Hall

Let us now return to our oversimplified auction hall and place it under the constraints of the Federal Reserve's debt system of money creation and introduction. Here we are, in a brand new auction hall. As of yet there is no "money" in it, and no "prices." But there is a Fed central bank in the auction hall, and whatever money that is to be used as a medium of exchange must be borrowed into general circulation from the Fed bank at 6 percent interest, compounded annually.

The merchants borrow $1,000 from the Fed bank. The auction hall opens for business. The bidding starts, and for the first time in the history of this brand new auction hall, "prices" begin to seek their levels against the volume of money floating about in it—$1,000.

Let us now imagine that twelve years have come and gone. Let us also imagine that both the principal and the interest on the public debt have been left unpaid in those twelve years ...

How much money is floating about in the auction hall? Still $1,000.

How much money do the merchants owe the central bank after twelve years? Answer: $2,012.

What would they have to do in order to be able to pay off their debt to the central bank right now? Raise the prices of their goods and services.

Granted, we are once again oversimplifying! And granted that within the framework of the existing Federal Reserve System, Uncle Sam need not worry about the principal—he only needs to keep up the interest payments. But we are, nevertheless, dealing with an existential *imbalance* here, an imbalance that is bound to effect the formulation of "prices" within the proverbial auction hall.

Let's look at the above example again. Twelve years ago, initial "prices" leveled themselves off against the $1,000 floating about in the auction hall. In those twelve years the amount of money floating in the auction hall has remained constant ($1,000). And let us assume the volume of goods and services in it has remained constant as well. But the debt has now swelled to $2,012. How is the auction hall going to compensate for the variable that has changed? By adjusting the remaining variable through systemic price inflation.

Look at it again. The volume of money floating about in the auction hall remains the same, but the volume of debt increases by geometric (compound) progression. This imbalance gives rise to systemic price inflation. Why?

It is not really difficult to see why! Look at it another way: the "taxpayers" in the auction hall would have to produce and bring to market goods and services in order to earn dollars, in order to pay taxes, in order to service their public debt. The longer the compound debt has been left to snowball, the more "dollars" in goods and services it will take to service the public debt.

Just as the cost of energy is an overhead of industry and commerce, the "cost" of money is a fundamental (but often overlooked) overhead of government and the private sector alike. In order to keep itself afloat, government will have to raise the ceiling on the national debt and tax the people accordingly. In order to keep themselves afloat, the people will have to raise their "prices." As the debt-overhead of the economy increases, the tax-paying manufacturer, faced with increases in his overhead, will be forced to raise the "price" of his products or go out of business. Similarly the manufacturer's workers, faced with increases in their cost of living, will have to demand higher wages or go broke. So begins the insidious cycle.

Systemic versus Classic Price Inflation

Systemic price inflation is not caused by an imbalance between volume of money floating about in the auction hall and volume of goods and services being traded in it ("too much money, chasing too few goods and services"). Systemic price inflation is caused by an imbalance between the volume of money floating in the auction hall and volume of associated debt—too little money, chasing too much debt.

Every economist knows (or should know) that classic price inflation is generally identifiable by the presence of *high levels of effective demand*. As we have already mentioned, this was the case with some of the OPEC nations a few decades ago where the glut of incoming oil money was producing high levels of effective demand, in turn resulting in the stampede to buy the few goods available on the shelves, in turn resulting in the auctioneers bidding up prices. But is this what is causing the underlying rate of inflation in America today—too much money, chasing too few goods and services? How would we be able to tell the difference between classic price inflation, and systemic price inflation? What would be the telltale sign of each? What would be the means of identification?

Telltale Sign of Classic Price Inflation

The telltale sign of classic price inflation would again have to be high levels of effective demand. Meaning what? Meaning there would be lots of money floating about in the auction hall. Meaning people would have lots of money in their pockets. Meaning people would want to buy lots of things, but there would not be enough things for them to buy. In which case the auctioneers would succeed in bidding up the prices of the little that there was for people to buy. Too much money, chasing too few goods and services!

Telltale Sign of Systemic Price Inflation

The telltale sign of systemic price inflation would have to be low levels of effective demand. Meaning what? Meaning prices would be seen to be rising *in spite of a sluggish economy*! Meaning what? Meaning people would not have enough money in their pockets to buy things. Meaning goods and services would be collecting dust on the shelves. In which case what? In which case you would expect to see auctioneers settling for *lower* prices in order to move things off the shelves. In which case what? In which case you would expect to see general prices coming *down*. Instead, however, you are seeing general prices rising.

We are again oversimplifying to drive home the point. With classic price inflation we would expect to see high levels of effective demand—lots of unencumbered money in people's pockets and the rush to buy the few goods and services remaining on the shelves. However, with systemic price inflation we would expect to see low levels of effective demand—hardly any unencumbered money in people's pockets, a sluggish economy, high unemployment, and no rush to buy anything. Yet prices keep rising steadily. How is that possible? What's the explanation?

There is only one explanation: we are dealing with a type of inflation that is built into the system itself.

Is there a glut of unencumbered money floating about in the auction halls of the American economy today? Are there too few goods and services on the shelves? Or is there in fact a grave shortage of unencumbered money floating about in the auction hall of the American economy today, causing people to avail themselves of the goods and services they need via unprecedented levels of credit card debt?

Unless we are willing to deny the evidence of our senses, every sign would seem to be warning us that, basically speaking, there is a grave shortage of money in the auction halls of the American economy today. Personal bankruptcies have reached epidemic proportions. On the heels of every hope looms the threat of default and mortgage foreclosure. Middle-class salaries are slashed. Pension plans are looted. Budgets are cut. The unemployment lines stretch from Maine to California. Millions are living below the poverty line. Every dollar is being stretched to the limit. Cities are teetering on the edge of bankruptcy. Uncle Sam himself is gnawing at the taxpayers' bones. And economists still want us to believe our underlying rate of inflation is caused by "too much money, chasing too few goods and services"?

No, we don't have to waste time trying to prove there is not nearly enough money floating about in the proverbial auction halls of the American economy to meet the monumental needs of a nation such as ours, a nation with several states that are in themselves among the highest ranking industrial entities in the world. Effective demand is low! The economy is sluggish. Manufacturers are offering cash incentives and large rebates just to lure buyers into their showrooms. And general prices still keep rising? How is this possible?

Stagflation

Economists will try to answer the question by waving their hands in the air, labeling the conundrum "stagflation," and immediately changing the subject. But the question remains.

By what sophistry of reason can a stagnant economy with record unemployment be said to be producing classic price inflation? By what rule of logic and divination can economists arrive at the conclusion that low levels of effective demand coupled with sky-high rates of unemployment can go hand in hand with steady *rises* in general prices?

Low levels of effective demand and high levels of unemployment would tend to produce classic price deflation, not inflation. There is something terribly wrong with this picture.

We are looking at a picture in which people are in debt up to their ears, struggling to keep body and soul together, have barely enough money to put food on the table and a roof over their children's heads, and have little or nothing left over for discretionary spending. Yet general prices continue creeping upward? We are looking at an auction hall in which effective demand has all but tanked, goods are collecting dust on the shelves, auctioneers are standing around with hopeless, hapless looks on their faces—and prices continue to rise? How is this possible? (Let the economic "experts" try to answer this question without throwing up smokescreens of convoluted jargon.)

Developed Nations

A nation is said to be "developed" when it has reached a certain plateau of industrial and technological maturity beyond which the fluent production of goods is no longer an obstacle to material abundance. Stated otherwise, the productive capacity of a developed nation such as the United States is such that it renders its economy progressively immune to the occurrence of classic price inflation. Why? Because the engine of the economy can speed up and crank out thousands of "new violins" to offset the increases in the volume of money floating about in the proverbial auction hall. Those rapid increases in the numbers of "new violins" for sale would quickly catch up to match, balance and equalize the increase in the volume of money, thus there would not be *too much* money, chasing *too few* "violins," in which case there would be no classic price inflation to speak of.

Yet our economic "experts" still like to maintain that the underlying rate of inflation in America is caused by *too much money* chasing *too few goods and services*? Astonishing and difficult to believe!

The term "anachronism" would be highly appropriate here. How, we ask, can it be said of a highly developed and advanced economy such as that of the United States that it is incapable of increasing its production of goods and services to balance and equalize relatively bucketfuls of increases in its basic money supply?

How can it be said of a nation whose commercial market dominates world trade, whose productive capacity is the linchpin of the hinge of the world's economy, a nation that went from Kitty Hawk to a manned lunar module on the moon in seventy years—how in heaven's name can it be said of such a nation that relatively pitiful increases in its basic money supply are more than what it can offset and equalize in the production of new goods and services?

The economists' jargon—too much money, chasing too few goods and services—may have been applicable during the horse and buggy era, and it may even have been applicable up to the time when Henry Ford was making Model As. Today, however, it is a ludicrous anachronism! Imagine, if you will, drastically curtailing the nation's supply of electricity, causing severe blackouts from coast to coast, and then trying to justify the policy on grounds that "there are not enough incandescent lamps in existence to warrant the output of so much electricity."

Long ago, ease of production ceased to be an obstacle to material prosperity in America. We the People have not had any trouble producing for many decades now, and today our ability to produce goods and services knows no bounds. It is not the failure to produce goods and services that has brought about the underlying cancer of inflation. It is the failure of the US Congress to address and correct the monumental mistake that it made when it passed the Federal Reserve Act of 1913.

Now we do not deny that the total inflation picture in America is a jumbled mess indeed. How shall it be described? How shall it be comprehended? Yes, as the supply of debt money periodically swells, the auctioneers succeed in bidding up prices, and we may be dealing with the ephemeral symptoms of classic price inflation. But the ephemeral symptoms don't give us the whole picture. They merely mask the nature of the underlying cancer.

Yes, the overall inflation picture in America is convoluted. Yes, the American auction hall is not a closed system. Yes, there are vast amounts of money sloshing in and out of it daily. Yes, there is capital entering it from the sale of bonds to Germany or China, for example. Yes, there is capital flying out of it because of the trade deficit.

Add to this already convoluted picture the machinations in currency markets, the gambling in futures and options markets, the lingering paroxysms of the subprime mortgage meltdown, the billions in bailouts, the fluctuations in the price of a barrel of crude oil, the massive proliferation of credit card debts, the epileptic spasms of the stock market, the coffin trades and bet-to-fail shenanigans of Wall Street ... and the overall picture deteriorates to a misshapen hodgepodge twisted enough to bring about the onset of intellectual paralysis.

The Federal Reserve Policy

What is causing the *underlying* rate of inflation in America and the developed world today? Is it classic price inflation? Or is it systemic price inflation? Are central bankers even aware of the existence of systemic price inflation? Is it conceivable that the economic "experts" of our own Federal Reserve System, the Bank of England, the European Central Bank, the World Bank and the International Monetary Fund are altogether oblivious with respect to the mechanism of systemic price inflation?

Now we do not deny that the Federal Reserve policy of "tightening credit" can keep a lid on prices. On the face of it, the Fed can *appear* to be "controlling inflation" by raising interest rates, thereby reducing the volume of money floating about in the proverbial auction hall, and, temporarily, keeping a lid on rising prices.

A typical scenario might go like this: The Fed, whose messianic duty is to "control inflation," makes a proclamation to the effect that it has detected "inflationary pressures." The Fed raises the "discount rate." The commercial banks in turn raise their interest rates. Fewer merchants can now afford to borrow money into general circulation. The volume of money in the proverbial auction hall is temporarily reduced. There is less money floating about in people's pockets, and the auctioneers have to settle for lower prices. Trade and commerce begin to stagnate. Merchants end up selling fewer goods. The bulls retire for a while. The bears come out of their closets. The economy languishes. The unemployment rolls increase. Tax revenues decrease.

The Congress wants to know what is going on. The Congress summons the chairman of the Federal Reserve to a hearing on the state of the American economy. "What is the Fed doing?" the congressman asks. The Fed chairman replies, "We are doing our job! We are controlling inflation!"

Is the Federal Reserve policy of raising interest rates going to cure the underlying cancer? Or is it just a clever way of imposing wage and price controls? Is it going to fix the problem? Or is it going to mask it from now until doomsday?

The first and most important step toward curing inflation is correct diagnosis. When we go and confuse classic price inflation with systemic price inflation—when we attempt to deal with the cancer on the false premise that it is just a rash—we have gone a long way toward defeating ourselves. We can pretend the cancer is a rash and try to "control" it by reducing the volume of money floating about in the auction hall. We can "raise interest rates," "tighten credit," and squeeze the pockets of the people in the auction hall from now until doomsday, but the cancer will not go away. It will get worse instead.

It is astonishing and difficult to believe, but here's what's happened. Seeing the outward symptoms of inflation, and not willing to be bothered by the correct diagnosis, the "experts" who have assumed charge over our failing economy continue to believe the problem is being caused by *too much money chasing too few goods and services.* So they imagine the best course of action would be for the nation to swallow the bitter medicine and allow the central bankers to raise interest rates (in other words, to cure the cancer, strangle the patient).

Granted, in the wake of the economic catastrophes that were triggered by the recent subprime mortgage meltdown, the Fed has been obliged to be very generous with interest rates, even reducing them to historically low levels. We can rest assured, however, that this is a temporary reprieve. We can rest assured that as soon as the American economy gets back on its feet—as soon as the unemployment figures return to "normal" levels—the Fed will want to return to its old tricks. It will again announce that it has detected the return of "inflationary pressures." And then it will raise the interest rates, giving the American economy another devastating blow in the ribcage.

How many times does this charade have to repeat itself before We the People wake up from the sleep of the dead and replace the seventeenth-century scaffolding that is the harbinger of systemic price inflation?

Raising interest rates in order to cure systemic price inflation is a flawed policy based on a flawed diagnosis. An analogy might be sought to show the folly of such a policy. Imagine, if you will, that there has been a flash flood in August. And imagine a survivor of that flood, stranded waist deep in contaminated, murky flood waters, suffering from heat exposure and thirst. He sees the members of the Open Market Committee of the Federal Reserve approaching in a rescue boat. Overjoyed, he cries out, "Water! Give me some water!"

The members of the Open Market Committee survey his condition, withdraw, and discuss it amongst themselves. Then, with a great show of paternal scholarship and wisdom, they issue the following statement of Fed policy: "Water? You want water? No! No! We must not give you any! There is too much of it in circulation already! It will worsen your condition!"

Chapter 10

The God of Gold:
The Accursed Lust

So all the people took off the rings of gold which were in their ears, and brought them to Aaron. And he received the gold at their hand ... and made a molten calf; and they said, "These are your gods, O Israel, who brought you up out of the land of Egypt."—Exodus 32:3–5 (RSV)

Falsehood is to be most feared when it mingles with some form of truth. Inasmuch as it has involved itself with truth, it begins to lay claim to the truth, and the half-truth thus created greatly increases the power of the falsehood. Among the half-truths that cause people to believe they are embracing some truth is one that may read something like this: unless a nation's money is backed with gold, it will be no good!

People have heard this half-truth so many times they have been conditioned into believing it is an original idea, a basic principle, a sound rule, an established axiom of money and finance. It is not uncommon to find the most sensible of our senior citizens casting disdainful glances at the government and making statements that may go something like this: "If only Nixon had not taken us off the gold standard!" or, "If only our money had been backed up with gold, we wouldn't be in the mess we're now in!"

To be sure, in archaic times mutual trust between trading partners could not be taken for granted, so it became expedient to use a medium of exchange that was rare and precious enough to have intrinsic value at all times and in all places without the force of law. However, as the archaic modes of exchange began to be replaced by greater degrees of civilization, as the concepts of "government" and "contract law" matured to the point where agreements and business promises became legally binding, the need for the archaic practice of using gold, silver, and metallic denominators of exchange "with fixity of value" was increasingly phased out.

Today, the only thing a civilized nation need do to provide its people with a lawful medium of exchange is see to it that its issuance is just, fair, and equitable, and that the law of the land declares it *receivable at its face value for payment of all debts, public and private, and all taxes, fees, and other charges due the government.*

The legal formality aside, the most important thing money needs to be backed up with is the real wealth and productive capacity of the nation issuing it. Thus we might say the integrity of the US dollar lies in the capacity of the American people at all times to receive and honor it—in exchange for its face value—in terms of goods and services. To burden coin or currency with "stores of value" in this day and age is anachronistic. Moreover, it is a waste of rare metals that could be put to better use.

The Charter of the Bank of England in 1694

Perhaps we should digress briefly to mention that prior to the charter of the Bank of England in 1694, a state-sanctioned debt system of money creation and introduction was for the most part unknown in the Western world. For example, before 1694, "tallies" were commonly used as money by the English people. First adopted by Henry the First (also known as *Henry Beauclerc,* King of England from 1100 to 1135), the acceptability of the tallies as media of exchange was mainly derived from the fact that they were *receivable for payment of taxes.*

The system was basically debt free and worked like this. The tallies, looking like short rods made of durable hardwood, were carefully marked with notches (indicating denominations, etc.) and then split lengthwise. One half was kept in the king's treasury, and the other half was *paid* into general circulation free of debt and interest when the crown needed to buy something. The pattern and intervals between the intricate notches along with the natural irregularities associated with different pieces of wood assured that only the original two halves would fit perfectly, safeguarding against forgeries. When returned to the treasury in payment of taxes, the outbound half was compared with the treasury half. If the two halves matched and mated exactly, the king's treasurer would cry "Tally ho!" and accept the returned half in payment of taxes.

Little by way of associated public debts were incurred in the course of the centuries during which the tallies circulated as money, or as IOUs, or as other promises to pay. When the Bank of England (also known as the *Old Lady of Threadneedle Street*) was chartered in 1694, there was about $70 million of wooden tallies in circulation. The new Bank was then accorded the privilege and monopoly of creating and introducing paper money into circulation within the context and framework of a debt system (what we have been referring to as "seventeenth-century scaffolding of central banking"). Predictably the use of the more convenient paper money soon replaced the use of the wooden tallies.

In 1783 the use of wooden tallies as media of exchange was abolished by an act of the British Parliament. In 1830 piles of broken, worn out and rotting tallies were ordered to be secretly burned in a stove in the House of Lords. Interestingly enough, a defective chimney set fire to some paneling, which spread and resulted in the historic 1835 fire that completely destroyed the Houses of Parliament!

The Old Lady of Threadneedle Street

It is worth noting that prior to the charter of the *Old Lady of Threadneedle Street* (slang for the Bank of England), the English people had a basically viable system of money creation and introduction. The British Crown circulated the tallies when it wanted to purchase something from the people, and then recalled some of them in the form of taxes. Granted, the system was cumbersome and not perfect by any stretch of the imagination. But, in principle at least, it was a viable money-concept that was in use for six centuries, during which it produced little by way of public debt. It is also worth noting that in the span of time between the charter of the Bank of England in 1694 and the abolition of the wooden tallies in 1783, the monetary "worth" and "value" of the tallies was not questioned by the governors of the Bank of England.

The tallies were spirited out of existence by the privately owned Bank of England when it became the first legal purveyor and executor of a centralized debt system of money creation. Truth be told, all of the central banks of the world today, including our own Federal Reserve Banks, bear upon their gilded and marbled foreheads the method, mark, and spirit of the *Old Lady of Threadneedle Street*. (And in this we are again saying that the seventeenth-century scaffolding is old and obsolete!)

The Young American Colonies

Keeping in mind the business with the charter of the Bank of England in 1694, let us now fast forward to the plight of the young American colonies in 1775. It was a troubled time, a time of Revolution! In fighting the greatest imperial, colonial, naval, and financial power in the world (Great Britain), the Founding Fathers of America had to find a way to feed, equip, and pay the patriot army. There was no established form of money, only varying forms of barter, here and there supplemented by a hodgepodge of European coins, notes, IOUs, and promises to pay, the conventions and usages of which differed from colony to colony.

The young American colonies had little by way of gold or silver. They could not levy taxes on the citizenry (the colonies had yet to unite into a single nation). They were considered a band of rebels, so no self-respecting nation would have loaned them money. The only thing they could do was print their own money and *pay* it into circulation free of debt and interest—*pay* the soldiers, *pay* the feed suppliers, *pay* the gunsmiths, *pay* the ironmongers, *pay* the carpenters, *pay* the cooper, *pay* the horseshoe maker, etc. Which they did.

In 1775 the first issue of Continental currency was printed by the firm *Hall & Sellers* in Philadelphia. Initially it proved itself a blessing. But it was not difficult to counterfeit.

Naturally, it didn't take long for the Tories and the board of governors of the Bank of England to hear about this shocking development! Alarmed by the news that the American Colonies had not only dared create their *own* money but actually had the gall to introduce it into general circulation *free of debt and interest*, they rushed to inform King George. If the American colonies were allowed to prosper by creating their own debt-free money, why would they want to remain satellites of the British Empire? Why would *any* of the British colonies want to remain loyal to the Crown if they could do the same thing? And why would any of them want to continue paying the taxes levied by the British Crown? No! This sort of thing was simply unacceptable. They had to do something about it. And they did.

The Crown, the Tories—and undoubtedly the governors of the Old Lady of Threadneedle Street—undertook a clandestine effort to render the Continental currency worthless by flooding the American colonies with counterfeits bills. The British general Sir William Howe was placed in charge of the counterfeiting operation, which shortly helped destroy the purchasing power of the Continental currency, giving rise to the colonial-era aphorism, "Not worth a Continental!"

In his newly published work *Common Sense*, then American patriot Thomas Paine was none too kind in excoriating the British general for the dastardly deed:

> To argue with a man who has renounced the use and authority of reason, and whose philosophy consists in holding humanity in contempt, is like administering medicine to the dead, or endeavoring to convert an atheist by scripture ...
>
> Mankind are not universally agreed in their determination of right and wrong; but there are certain actions which the consent of all nations and individuals hath branded with the unchangeable name of *meanness*. In the list of human vices we find some of such refined constitution, that they cannot be carried into practice without seducing some virtue to their assistance; but *meanness* hath neither alliance nor apology.... Sir William, the commissioner of George the Third, hath at last vouchsafed to give it rank and pedigree. He has placed the fugitive at the council board and dubbed it companion of the order of knighthood.
>
> The particular act of meanness which I allude to in this description, is forgery. You, sir, have abetted and patronized the forging and uttering [of] counterfeit continental bills. In the same New York newspapers in which your own proclamation under your master's authority was published, offering, or pretending to offer, pardon and protection to the inhabitants of these colonies, there were repeated advertisements of

counterfeit money for sale, and persons who have come officially from you and under sanction of your flag, have been taken up [arrested] in attempting to put them off.

A conduct so basely mean in a public character is without precedent or pretence. Every nation on earth, whether friends or enemies, will unite in despising you. 'Tis an incendiary war upon society which nothing can excuse or palliate—an improvement upon beggarly villainy—and shews an inbred wretchedness of heart made up between the venomous malignity of a serpent and the spiteful imbecility of an inferior reptile.

The laws of any civilized country would condemn you to the gibbet without regard to your rank or titles, because it is an action foreign to the usage and custom of war; and should you fall into our hands, which pray God you may, it will be a doubtful matter whether we are to consider you as a military prisoner or a prisoner of felony.[18]

The Wording of the Constitution

Some will no doubt point to the wording found in Article 1, Section 8, Paragraph 5 of the Constitution, ostensibly equating money with "coins." What then? What are we to think? Where the words read, "Congress shall have power to ... coin money and regulate the value thereof ...," are we to understand that the Constitution empowers the Congress to create US dollars in coins but not US dollars in bills?

Now we might accede that the Constitution was drawn up at a troubled time when the whole issue of paper money had been thrown in doubt by the negative and abortive experience of the young American colonies with respect to the forging of the Continental currency. We would emphatically deny, however, that in this, or in any other respect, the Constitution limits the prerogative of US Congress to the creation of metal coins alone! It is absurd to maintain that the Constitution empowers the Congress to create dollars in coins but not dollar bills. Common sense alone would indicate

---

[18] Thomas Paine, *Common Sense: The Rights of Man and other Essential Writings*, with an introduction by Sidney Hook (New York: Penguin Books, 1969), 88–91.

the following: Where the Constitution says, "Congress shall have power to coin money," it means "Congress shall have power to create a just, fair, and equitable medium of exchange for use in trade and commerce."

Hepburn v. Griswold, 1867

Under the Legal Tender Act of 1862, President Abraham Lincoln ordered the Bureau of Printing and Engraving to issue $450 million in greenbacks, and then he *paid* it into general circulation free of debt and interest. The president himself did not see in the Constitution any limit to that issue of paper currency, and the Congress did not oppose him.

In 1867 the case of *Hepburn v. Griswold*, challenging the Legal Tender Act of 1862, was taken up by the Supreme Court. Lawyers acting on behalf of the bullion brokers argued that if in 1861 the government had promised to pay its debts in gold, it could not thereafter turn around and pay its debts in paper greenbacks. In deciding the case, the justices were initially divided. Eventually, however, they declared the Legal Tender Act of 1862 to be constitutional, Justice Strong arguing that it helped pay for the Civil War and save the nation. Justice Miller added the following:

> A general collapse of credit, of payment, and of business seemed inevitable ... faith in the government would have been destroyed, the rebellion would have triumphed, the States would have been left divided, and the people impoverished. The National Government would have perished, and with it, the Constitution. ... The Legal Tender Act prevented these disastrous results. ... It furnished instantly a means of paying the soldiers in the field. ... It stimulated trade, revived the drooping energies of the country, and restored confidence to the public mind.[19]

There is no rational ground to interpret Article 1, Section 8, Paragraph 5 of the Constitution as limiting the power of Congress to the creation

---

[19] Justice Miller, dissenting, *Hepburn v. Griswold, 1870*. US Supreme Court cases, from volume 75 of the *United States Report*, citation 75 US 603, paragraph 97.

of "metallic coins" alone. The industrial and technological leaps that have taken the nation from the horse-and-buggy era to the space age have now rendered the entire concept of "money metalism" barbaric.

Gold Backing

Money is the lifeblood of the physical economy. There must at all times be a sufficient amount of it in circulation to meet the legitimate needs of industry and commerce. If a nation's money is to be backed up with gold, then the availability of gold will dictate the boundaries of prosperity and progress. This is itself an abhorrent thought, to say nothing of the extortion that mankind will probably end up having to endure under the whip of whatever cabal or syndicate that may happen to be controlling the world's supplies of gold at the time. And what if the world runs out of gold? What shall we do then? Stand about in the unemployment lines and wait for someone to find gold on the moon?

There is not enough gold in the entire world to back up the currencies of a few industrialized nations, let alone the currencies of all nations at the same time. Imagine a barbaric scenario in which a more powerful nation was faced with one of two choices: either to attack (buy up) the gold bases of a weaker nation, or to curtail its own livelihood in order to preserve the sacrosanct ratio between gold and money—and endure with dumb anguish the resulting poverty, unemployment, and unrest.

If the "standby" for the protection of currency is to be gold (instead of other useful wealth *produced* by the nation), then gold will become the stumbling block of trade, and those who control it will become the amateur gods of industry and commerce. One does not need to be a prophet to see that a global monetary system based on gold would, by natural progress, tend to yield itself to the lowest denominator of human nature in barbarism of every description.

If we were shipwrecked on a barren island literally made of gold and silver, neither ten tons of gold nor a hundred tons of silver would have as much "value" as a loaf of bread to eat or a good book to read! The only reason gold is able to command its high "value" is because it is a *rare* commodity. If gold is to be used in world trade because it is a rare metal and hence able to retain some sort of "intrinsic value," then trade wars are inevitable because there isn't enough of it to back up the currencies of all nations. And we don't have to waste time proving that a trade war is often the prelude to a shooting war.

On the other hand, if there were major discoveries of gold, enough to back up the currencies of all nations at the same time, then it would no longer be a rare metal, would it? And if no longer a rare metal, how would it retain its intrinsically high value? So then why not use another metal in that case, one that is already abundant, say, copper, to back up the currencies of the whole world? Absurd, you say? Yet it is just as absurd to say that the money of the world must be backed up with gold!

If backward nations demand to be paid in pure gold, let them do so to their own shame and depravity. But in heaven's name, let us not have the government of the United States engage in the idolatrous practice of treating gold as though it had arcane and supernatural properties, or to engage in the idolatrous practice of declaring gold to have an artificial "legal tender value" that is different from its commodity value.

In the beginning of this chapter we pointed out that the power of error is often made most detrimental when it mixes itself with some measure of truth. For inasmuch as the error has involved itself with truth, it begins to lay claim to the truth, and the half-truth thus created greatly increases the power of error. Case in point, the so-called "need" to back up paper money with gold.

All too often we may hear some well-intentioned but misguided soul in the media lift up his or her voice in favor of a restoration of the "gold standard." All too often we may run into plausible-sounding editorials in newspapers, any one of which may read something like this: "When a nation's money supply is backed up with gold, there is a built-in restraint against politicians printing too much paper money." Such an editorial opinion is a prime example of how a half-truth can delude people into believing they are embracing some token of truth and virtue. The very mention of the word "restraint," followed by "politicians" and "paper money" is enough to pull the wool over the eyes of the Congress, the White House, and the Supreme Court alike.

At first glance such an editorial opinion would appear to be pregnant with all of the elements of virtue and wisdom, implying, for example, that if "the greedy politicians" were forced to back up their "paper dollars" with gold, they would be "restrained" and "disciplined" from "going down in the basement and printing too much of it," thereby causing runaway, classic price inflation.

In the first place we have already pointed out that, under the guidelines of the Federal Reserve Act of 1913 politicians are not allowed to "go down in the basement and print money," only central bankers are allowed to do that. Under those guidelines, politicians can only print debt in the form of bonds, and then use those bonds as the collateral to *borrow* new money into general circulation from the central banks (or from other nations).

In the second place, we have gone to some lengths to show that the long-term, chronic inflation that has been eroding the purchasing power of the dollar since 1913 cannot possibly be of the classic variety, caused by the politicians' unbridled lust for "printing-press money." We have gone to some pains to show that the *underlying* cancer that has been eating up the substance of the US dollar is systemic—built into the Federal Reserve System itself.

Money is simply a convenient medium of exchange. It has no intrinsic value and needs no "metallic store of value." The only thing money does need to be backed up with is the real wealth and productive capacity of the nation in which it is being used as a medium of exchange.

In a truly civilized society, a plastic dollar would serve the same purpose as one made of pure gold. Why? Because it is just a medium of exchange and the element that makes it "good" is the faith and credit of We the People in its reliable purchasing power.

There is no law that says, "Unless printed money is backed up with gold, it will end up being worthless." There is no such law, no such axiom, no such rule of economic logic and divination. This is just another one of those carelessly accepted superstitions that would make a fetish out of gold and gods out of those who control its supplies.

Chapter 11

Money Myths and Superstitions:
A Closet Full of Half-Truths

It is more from carelessness about the truth, than from intention of lying, that there is so much falsehood in the world.—Samuel Johnson

Even a cursory glance at the mythology that hangs about our money system like a fog will reveal a hodgepodge of myths and ideas, assumed to be true and applied as hard and fast rules, but for what reason no one seems to know. In the preceding chapters we have discussed some of the more egregious of these superstitions. We must now expose the remaining ones.

"Wartime Economy"

One fallacy that seems to have embedded itself into the public mind has to do with the idea that wars make for prosperous economies. In this connection we may still find some editorials referring to brief periods of American prosperity and full employment, but then qualifying those opinions by adding something like this: "Ah yes, but that was during a wartime economy."

The implication of such a statement is that if a nation wants to revive its economy, the quickest way would be to "cry havoc and let slip the dogs of war" (Shakespeare, *Hamlet*). This is in itself an abhorrent sentiment. So now we must ask, Who says wars make for prosperous economies?

Regardless of whether a war is justified, when a nation gets itself embroiled in one, this is what happens: The government in effect declares a state of emergency and *borrows* a great deal more money from central banks than it normally would. The increase in the volume of money then causes industrial activity to temporarily surge, which causes the unemployment figures to come down, tax revenues to go up, etc. But the plain fact is that the same increase in industrial activity, employment, and tax revenues would take place if the money supply were increased for any other reason.

Again, money is the lifeblood of industry and commerce. If the lifeblood is curtailed, the economy will stagnate. If the lifeblood is increased, the economy will speed up. It is not the wartime circumstance that revives the economy. The economy is revived for one reason only: the increase in volume of money.

If a sovereign government such as that of the United States can find within itself the authority to revive the economy by increasing purchasing power in times of war, it can also find within itself the authority to revive the economy by increasing purchasing power in times of peace. It takes as much money to finance the manufacture of the provisions of life and construction as it does to manufacture the munitions of death and destruction. In both cases materials must be bought, industries must be revived and retooled, salaries must be paid, etc. So what's the problem?

Perhaps part of the problem is again rooted in human nature itself. Where there is peace, prosperity, abundance, and plenty, little can be held in ransom. Where there is crisis, conflict, and scarcity, that is where the shortcomings associated with human nature find ground to thrive on.

The power to grant or withhold credit to or from sovereign nations is god-like in scope and dimension. And when money is rendered scarce, it tends to increase the power of those who are in a position to grant or withhold it. The central banking institutions that have been exercising this sort of god-like power for about three hundred years are run by mortal and fallible human beings. Given the choice between financing the munitions of war and destruction or financing the provisions of life and construction, which do you think they would tend to choose? The answer, no doubt, has to do with some quirk or foible common to all mankind regardless of race, color, creed, or nationality. And here we do not exclude ourselves from that pejorative!

We have already ascertained that a strong economy is in itself an essential condition of liberty and guarantee of peace. Now, if a strong economy is an essential condition of liberty and guarantee of peace, it is reasonable to assume that a weak economy would tend to be the opposite—the breeding ground of oppression, conflict, and war.

When there is a legitimate threat to national security, a government may mobilize its resources and go to war to remove that threat. What then? Is there no threat to national security associated with a weak and failing economy?

What about this national debt that hangs over our heads and the heads of our children and grandchildren like the sword of Damocles? What about the horrendous deficits that paralyze our initiatives and make America appear weak and impotent in the sight of the world? What about the systemic inflation that is sapping the nation's vitality? What about the unemployment lines stretching from Maine to California? What about the ever- increasing number of bank failures? What about the epidemic of personal bankruptcies? What about the cities of America teetering on the edge of bankruptcy? What about pollution, congestion, and waste? What about the revolving door of crime? What about the overcrowded prisons? Is there no threat to national security in all this?

"Periodic Recessions Are Necessary"

Another of those amazing theories that are nowadays accepted because they are seldom challenged has to do with the idea of the "inevitability" of major ups and downs in the economy. In this connection we may find editorial opinions that attempt to explain the periodic spasms of the American economy as though the events were inevitable and unavoidable.

So-called economic "experts" and Wall Street pundits are comfortable making statements that may go something like this: "Yes, well, after two boom years, the economy was due for a downturn." Here is a statement that should be dismissed as a masterpiece of ambiguity, or at least investigated a little. Sad to say, however, such statements are nowadays accepted without question on Wall Street and in the mainstream media. They are accepted as part and parcel of an esoteric religion of "money," a belief system subscribed to by a nervous subculture of financial fortunetellers whose entire stock and trade consists of trying to make money with money.

111

They sit all day, gazing into their crystal balls, trying to conjure up the telltale signs of a coming "panic" or "credit event." If they think they have found those telltales signs, and if the business cycles, the dice, the phases of the moon, and the signs of the Zodiac so portend, they may conclude that the recovery has "peaked out" and the market is now "due for a correction." At this time, one of them will press the panic button, and the ensuing stampede will send speculators trampling over hill and dale in the desperate effort to convert their "volatile assets" into "liquidity"—"Sell! Sell! Sell!"

Now we would not deny that we live in a world in which *minor* economic ups and downs may be experienced from time to time. However, we would disagree with those who would have us believe the *major* ups and downs that have plagued the American economy are "inevitable" or "unavoidable."

Let us now stop to question and investigate this assumption. Who says that after a few boom years the economy will be due for a downturn? Just what sort of reasoning is this? Upon what premise, what axiom, what rule of logic and divination is this nonsense based? By what sophistry of reason should a few years of prosperity *necessarily* have to be followed by a period of recession or let-down? And why in heaven's name should the American economy have to produce *any* recessions in the first place?

We have already explained that given the framework of the three-hundred-year-old debt system, there is no permanent money supply to speak of. Rather, the whole of the economy has to depend on the "put-out and take-back" nature of the debt system. Given this degree of dependency on the ephemeral nature of debt money, and given the shortcomings associated with human nature itself, it is within these contexts that periodic stagnations of the American economy become predictable and inevitable.

When money is rendered scarce it tends to increase the power of those who create and control it. Be it by reason of human nature itself or by reason of the *hemorrhage* that we discussed previously (money bleeding out of the auction hall to service the debt), it is reasonable to assume that periodic scarcity will tend to become a rule of thumb in a debt system. The periodic scarcity of money will then translate into periodic lowering of effective demand, which will translate into periodic increases of unemployment, economic malaise, etc.

The reason the American economy gets sick once in a while has to do with curtailments of its life-sustaining blood. This is how it usually happens: the Fed will issue a statement to the effect that the economy has been "overextended" and the demand for credit has started to "outstrip" the nation's capacity to match it with the production of goods and services. This statement is usually followed by an edict, which may go something like this: "In order to keep a lid on inflationary pressures, it is now necessary to tighten up on credit."

And so the Fed raises the basic interest rates. And so the economy staggers and reels. And so the fortunetellers issue their opinions, any one of which may go something like this: "Yes, well, after gaining so many points in the last eighteen months, the stock market was long overdue for a major correction." Or something like this: "Yes, well, after two years of significant growth, the economy was due for a downturn." What manner of reasoning is this?

A reminder: money is the lifeblood of the economy. If that lifeblood is curtailed, the economy will stagnate. If that lifeblood is restored, the economy will revive. Either way, the economy does not go up and down because it is getting in and out of phase with some phantom cycle. It revives itself when granted its life-sustaining flow of money. It stagnates when denied its life-sustaining flow of money.

"We Are Spending Too Much"

The ease with which erroneous assumptions can be made with respect to the monetary role of government, and the extent to which central banks have succeeded in co-opting and usurping that role, is truly astonishing. Case in point, the bewildering statement made a few years ago by British Prime Minister Margaret Thatcher.

In March 1981, during the decade in which ideas about fiscal conservatism were resurgent in Great Britain and the United States alike, Mrs. Thatcher paid a visit to the United States, stood shoulder to shoulder with President Reagan, and in a televised speech made the following statement of policy with regard to deficit reduction: "We cannot go on spending more than the nation earns and printing the difference."

What's wrong with this picture?

When Mrs. Thatcher says, "We cannot go on spending more than the nation earns and *printing* the difference," she is unknowingly contradicting herself. The analogy that comes to mind is one of a severe famine in which a farmer is found to be making an equally contradictory statement: "We cannot go on promising more wheat than we produce and *planting* the difference."

We have already ascertained that money is a medium of exchange and that it is the responsibility and duty of every government to provide its people with a just, fair, and equitable medium of exchange. Mrs. Thatcher, however, seemed to be saying the British Government has been printing money—not to provide its people with a medium of exchange but in order to make up for the difference between what it earns from its tax revenues, and what it spends on social programs.

How is that possible? Is Mrs. Thatcher saying the debt-ridden British Government is, in part or in whole, depending on the money that it earns from its tax revenues to provide its people with a lawful medium of exchange? Was she saying the government was not earning enough money from tax revenues to provide its people with a lawful medium of exchange, so the government was printing money to make up for the difference?

What exactly was Mrs. Thatcher saying here?

If you, the reader, were in debt because you were spending more than you were earning, but could go down in your basement and print money to make up for the difference, would you still be in debt up to your ears?

If the British Government could print money to make up for the difference between what it was earning (from tax revenues) and what it was spending (on social programs, etc.), how could it be in debt up to its ears?

Is that in fact what the British Government has been doing—printing money to make up for the shortfall between spending and tax revenues? How is that possible? And since when did the United Kingdom become blessed with a debt-free system of money creation and introduction? Since when does the "Old Lady of Threadneedle Street" (the Bank of England) print money and just hand it over to the British Government so the British Government can make up for the difference between what it earns through tax revenues and what it spends on social programs?

Reality check. Any new money printed in England has to be *borrowed* into circulation, by the British Government, from the Bank of England! So then what Mrs. Thatcher meant to say, or should have said, is this: "We cannot go on spending more than the nation earns and borrowing the difference," which has a completely different meaning.

Notwithstanding, it has to be said that there is a deception afoot here, one that would, perhaps, unfairly blame and discredit legislators in the British Parliament and the US Congress alike. In chapter 5, a table showed the alarming way in which a compound debt will balloon if the principal is left untouched over the decades. It showed, for example, that if a debt of $1,000 were left unpaid for 48 years, it would take sixteen times as much money to pay it off, and if left unpaid for 120 years, it would take a thousand times as much money to pay it off.

Our own US national debt is now an astronomical figure in excess of $16 trillion. What does this mean? Does this mean that our elected representatives have "printed and spent" that much paper money? God forbid! Had that been the case, all the forests on earth would have been denuded by now for want of pulp to convert into "printing-press money."

Indeed, to see the colossal mountain of public debt confronting us, and to imagine that our public servants have "printed and spent" that much paper money, is a grand delusion. The truth is that no paper money has been "spent" into circulation by Congress since the Federal Reserve Act of 1913, and hardly any paper money has been "spent" into circulation by the British Government since the charter of the Bank of England in 1694. Rather, all of it has been borrowed into general circulation in the form of accumulative debt.

Now we do not dispute that there is waste in government. To be sure, there is, and as Senator Tom Coburn and other legislatures have shown, very serious amounts of it. And we do not disagree with those who would curb the evil tide of bureaucracy. Yes, the Founding Fathers did their best to safeguard the citizenry from the excesses of government. And no, it was not their intention to resurrect a new version of state paternalism with its infamous motto, "We know what is best for you." And no, it was not their intention to create a welfare state run by a legion of bureaucrats who love to spend the taxpayers' money.

At the same time, however, we would have our elected representatives know that our astronomical debts, horrendous deficits, and confiscatory taxation were not caused by too much "spending" in the holistic sense of the word. Rather, they were caused by too much borrowing. Our expanding economy and mushrooming technological base, together with our global mandates and responsibilities, demand that We the People spend money wisely, efficiently, and in due process of law. And the magnitude of our providential wealth should enable us to do so without drawing blank checks on future generations.

It has been estimated, for example, that the interest we now pay on our national debt for a single year is enough to finance the construction of two hundred Hoover Dams, with money left over to convert every state of the Union to solar, wind, geothermal, and steam power. Imagine what could be done in a debt-free system! Imagine the billions of dollars that would be left over for legitimate spending. Imagine balanced state and federal budgets. Imagine the possibilities! Imagine the transformation of America. Imagine the transformation of the world. Imagine the transcendent horizons and the limitless objectives that would then be within the reach of mankind. Think of the confidence it would restore. Think of the jobs.

"We Owe the National Debt to Ourselves"

Another fallacy that must be dispelled is the one that would have us believe we owe the national debt to ourselves. The idea that we owe the national debt to ourselves implies that since we don't have to ship money overseas or pay interest to "foreigners," there is no harm in having a national debt. Unfortunately, and even by this sort of Philistine reasoning, the fact is that a significant portion of our national debt is now in control of foreign entities.

When Congress prints debt in the form of bonds and securities, it may do one of two things with them. It may use them as the collateral to borrow new money into circulation from the Federal Reserve Banks. Alternately, it may "float" those bonds in the hope that someone (China, for example) will buy them. The bonds go from here to China. The money comes here from China. Uncle Sam pays interest to Chinese investors. Uncle Sam taxes us for those interest payments.

Is there cause for concern here? Well, let us remind ourselves that government bonds are evidence of a debt, the collateral for which is the very ground upon which we walk.

"The Fed Is Government Owned and Operated"

Speaking of myths and superstitions, some people also imagine that the twelve Federal Reserve Banks are somehow owned and operated by the US Government. The word "federal" evokes a vision of national authority, does it not? Unfortunately this too is a delusion. There is in reality nothing "federal" about the twelve Federal Reserve Banks.

The seven men that constitute the board of governors of the Federal Reserve are appointed by the president and have to be approved by the Senate. Unfortunately, the board of governors is not the same thing as the Federal Reserve Banks themselves, and it most certainly is not the same thing as the Open Market Committee of the Federal Reserve (FOMC).[20]

To say there has always been some controversy surrounding the constitutionality of the Federal Reserve System would be an understatement. In 1934, for example, Congressman Louis T. McFadden brought action before the judiciary for the impeachment of the Federal Reserve's directors for "criminal conspiracy," alleging that the Fed was an American arm of European banking oligarchies and that the whole thing amounted to the greatest crime in history. And, predictably, some people have been crying "conspiracy!" ever since.

Now whereas we would limit the issue to unwise legislation enacted in 1913 by members of Congress who are now dead, we would nevertheless be so bold as to enquire why there has never been a thorough investigation or audit of the Federal Reserve System. What are we to think? What are we to believe? Are we to believe there is indeed some truth to the "conspiracy"

---

[20] Within the framework of the Federal Reserve System, the Federal Open Market Committee (FOMC) controls the creation/introduction of new moneys and also oversees the marketing, trafficking, and trading of government securities. The FOMC, composed of the twelve central bankers (seven members of the Federal Reserve Board and five Federal Reserve Bank presidents) is the governing body of US monetary policy, making critical decisions about interest rates and monetary growth that impact the lives and fortunes of Americans. The FOMC also controls and presides over currency operations and trading undertaken by the Federal Reserve (in the name of the US Government) within foreign exchange markets.

hysteria? Are we to understand that the special interest that controls this so-called "money monopoly" is too powerful to allow any opposition to its privileged position to arise?

Now we bring all this to the attention of the American people not to alarm or incite them but to point the way toward genuine reform. In our open system of government, reform begins with public accountability, and we need only glance at our history to see this is so. More than one hundred Congresses have authorized investigations and exposed every public impropriety—malfeasance, iniquity, and injustice involving election scandals, questionable practices of railroads, utilities, oil companies, transportation, food and drug, insurance, shipping, steel, coal, housing, communications, etc.

From Teapot Dome to Watergate, Iran-Contra, and more recently, "Operation Fast and Furious," almost everything that impinges on the welfare of the American taxpayer, including the activities of the FBI and the CIA, have at various times been opened up to public scrutiny and congressional oversight. Through it all, however, one institution has managed to evade all attempts at full disclosure: the Fed, whose transactions involve billions upon billions of taxpayer dollars.

Now, whether the Federal Reserve Act of 1913 was actually constitutional, or whether it can be declared to have been *ultra vires* (overreaching the legal powers granted by the Constitution)[21] is something beyond the scope and purview of this publication (something that would have to be resolved in the courts). But here again, what are we to think? What are we supposed to believe? Here is a privately owned and operated central banking institution that calls itself "Federal Reserve." It creates debt money for the United States. It profits from the public debt of the United States. It has a power to grant or withhold credit to or from the United States. It has a power to design economic guidelines for the United States. And yet it will not confide in the US Congress?

Not only are central bankers allowed to freely pursue their vested multibillion-dollar interests in the unnecessary creation and increase of

---

[21] *Ultra Vires* (Latin, "beyond powers") is a legal term describing an official act (e.g., of the US Government) that requires legal authority (e.g. that of the Constitution) but is carried out without that authority. *Ultra vires* acts of the United States Government can be judged to be "invalid" and legally non-binding.

public debt, it would seem they have been given a free hand to determine their own legal privileges as well. How did that happen?

"Liberty, Motherhood, and Apple Pie"

Often the power of falsehood is made most detrimental when it mixes itself with some portion of truth, and among mankind's litany of historical errors, the most insidious are those that have managed to enlist some virtue to their support. Is it possible that the seventeenth-century scaffolding of central banking has managed to enlist American virtues to its support? Can a debt system of money creation and introduction be said to be the companion of American values, for example? Can it be said to be kith and kin to "motherhood and apple pie"? Can it be said to be sympathetic toward the liberty that we Americans hold near and dear to our hearts? Surely not! Liberty and bondage are as opposed as light and dark.

As mentioned previously, a man bound in debt is sometimes referred to as a bondsman, the person to whom he is bound is referred to as a bondholder, the document giving the latter a charge over the former is referred to as a bond, and the whole business is referred to as bondage. We Americans love to boast about our liberty, but we seem to have forgotten the inscription on the Liberty Bell in Philadelphia, a direct quote from Leviticus 25:10: "And you shall proclaim liberty throughout the land to all its inhabitants."

This passage of Scripture relates to a Mosaic law that set aside a "jubilee" every fifty years, during which the people were granted a general release from all debts! Perhaps this is why the great symbol of our American freedom—the Liberty Bell in Philadelphia—has a crack in it! The crack was repaired once, but it mysteriously reappeared. Without admitting to any superstition, one can only wonder if this may have something to do with the indignation harbored by the Supreme Judge of the Universe toward a people foolish enough to legalize a system based on perpetual debt, who then go and write "In God We Trust" on their money.

"As American as Private Property"

What about the notion that a debt system of money creation is as American as private property? Is that true? No it is not!

Government bonds are evidence of a debt, secured by a *mortgage*, which Webster's New World Dictionary defines as "the pledging of property to a creditor as security for the payment of a debt." Government bonds are, in this way, the taxpayers' promise to pay. We the People have to work, earn money, and pay the taxes that service our public debt. What happens if we don't pay those taxes? The government can confiscate our property and put us in jail. Considering that our national debt is now an astronomical figure in excess of $16 trillion, and bearing in mind that Congress is empowered to tax us to pay it off, it is not difficult to see the conflict between the seventeenth-century scaffolding of central banking and the private property rights of Americans.

Does the state own everything in America? Surely not! Yet if the Congressional abdication of monetary responsibility in 1913 is to be regarded as constitutional, it could be argued that the spirit of the Constitution is averse to the private property rights of individuals. But we know, as does every lawyer and judge, that the spirit and letter of the Constitution are supportive of the private property rights of individuals, and, in fact, bend over backward to guarantee those rights to citizens.

When the nation was young and in want of funds, Benjamin Franklin was sent to Europe to borrow money. When the Founding Fathers wrote in the Constitution, "Congress shall have power to ... borrow money on the credit of the United States," they meant just that. They did not mean to allow Congress to raise the national debt ceiling on a regular basis, and they most certainly did not have it in mind to empower Congress to mortgage the land to the point of national bankruptcy. This is a circumstance clearly in violation of the private property rights guaranteed to individuals by the Constitution.

"As American as Free Enterprise"

For reasons already mentioned, a debt system of money creation stifles free enterprise. Our American economy is obviously controlled by the central bankers that sit on the Open Market Committee of the Federal Reserve. A controlled economy is not quite the same thing as a free economy. If the free-enterprise system were allowed to function freely, our outlook would know no such things as cyclic recessions, horrendous deficits, astronomical debts, and systemic inflation!

Truth be told, we do not have *free* enterprise in America today, not in its true sense. All American free enterprise is under Fed control. All of it is at risk, depending on whether the Fed is going to be generous with interest rates for a season or whether it is going to raise them under the pretext of "controlling inflation."

"As American as Capitalism"

What about the idea that a debt system of money creation is as American as capitalism? Can that be true?

Christ said something that bears mentioning here: "For which of you, desiring to build a tower, does not first sit down and count the cost, whether he has enough to complete it? Otherwise, when he has laid a foundation, and is not able to finish, all who see it begin to mock him, saying, 'This man began to build, and was not able to finish'" (Luke 14:28–30, RSV).

No one starts a small business without first sitting down and doing the math to see if the business will turn a profit. If an entrepreneur does the math and decides the return on his investment will exceed the cost of borrowing, he may take out a business loan from the local bank and pay interest on it, and there is nothing wrong with that. If a corporation does the math and decides the return on its investment will exceed the cost of going public, it may issue stock and pay dividends to stockholders, and there is nothing wrong with that either. So what's the problem?

Here's the problem: just as the cost of energy is an overhead of industry and commerce, the cost of "money" is a fundamental (but often overlooked) overhead of government and the private sector alike.

What will the government have to do in order to keep up the ballooning interest payments on the national debt? Raise taxes. And what will the taxpaying private sector have to do in order to turn a profit and/or distribute dividends to stockholders? It will have to raise its prices.

121

Our public debt alone is a now a colossal figure in excess of $16 trillion! At what point will the fundamental overhead of government and private sector alike (the cost of money; the cost of servicing the debt) render taxation confiscatory and drive the prices of goods and services beyond the reach of people in the proverbial auction hall?

None of this is rocket science. Simply by projecting the compound curves into the future, we can clearly see that at some absurd point every cent businesses and corporations earn will have to be set aside for payment of debt-related taxes.

Private sector capital investments are based on anticipated returns. Unless adequate returns are forthcoming, no capital investment will be made by the private sector in the first place. And unless adequate dividends are forthcoming, no one will want to invest in the stock market either. So then what is all this vain talk about "capitalism"?

If by "capitalism" it is meant the traffic, bargain, and deception involved in the marketing of "securities" and falsifications of money—derivatives, short trades, put options, junk bonds, collateralized debt obligations, credit default swaps, coffin trades, and Wall Street's bet-to-fail shenanigans—then let it be accursed!

But if by "capitalism" it is meant private sector investments in the private ownership of the means of wealth creation, then it needs no prophet's eye to see that by taking capital out of physical economies, a debt system competes against the uniquely American concept of wealth creation.

Conclusion

A debt system of money creation and introduction is averse to the intent of America's founders. It stands in contempt of the spirit and letter of the Constitution. It is inimical with respect to the liberty that we Americans hold near and dear to our hearts. It is predatory with respect to private property. It is a stumbling block to free enterprise, and by its very nature preys on the sort of capital investments and corporate ownerships that have made this nation strong at the grassroots level of small businesses.

At the same time, and given the shortcomings associated with human nature itself, a debt system of money creation places those mortals who create and control the nation's credit in positions of unfair advantage from which they will, sooner or later, use the difficulties of the times to amass fortunes on the public ruin.

This is what a debt system of money creation is all about—all myths, superstitions, and plausible sophistries to the contrary notwithstanding.

Chapter 12

Millennial Economics:
The Sea Change to Debt-Free National Economies

Ho, every one who thirsts, come to the waters; and he who has no money, come, buy and eat! Come, buy wine and milk without money and without price. Why do you spend your money for that which is not bread, and your labor for that which does not satisfy?—Isaiah 55:1–2 (RSV).

The debt paradigm of money creation is now obsolete. It can no longer meet the current needs of the world, let alone meet its needs in the new millennium. Notwithstanding that it has mired the whole world in debt, notwithstanding that it is now competing against the labor of man and seeking to deprive him of the dignity of his origins in God, it is now also placing the future of the planet itself at risk.

The compromise of ecosystems; the pollution of the air, the rivers, and the oceans; the destruction of species; the decimation of forests; the depletion of resources; and the general degradation of God's green earth, in part or in whole, relate themselves to the issue of global debt.

Unless the obsolete paradigm is replaced, and soon, the world will carry the dead weight of the old order into the new millennium and there will be nothing in store but more of the same. More debt. More poverty. More scarcity. More want. More dependency. More tension. More conflict. More war. More pollution. More congestion. More waste. More disease. More mass misery. More death. The handwriting is on the wall, and the facts speak for themselves.

It is time for a sea change.

The economic "experts" of our age seem to be suffering from some sort of mental block. The few who see beyond the veil and are now calling for debt-free systems of money creation and introduction are as voices crying in the wilderness. While these voices are quick to point out the flaws of the existing system, they are slow in prescribing the one that will have to replace it. While they are eager to see the Federal Reserve System replaced with something better, they are in disagreement as to precisely what should take its place. Indeed, some of the "solutions" they propose reveal as great a confusion of ideas and thoughts as one can imagine. Perhaps this is because we have all lost sight of the fundamental causes that led to the invention of "money" in the first place.

Back to the Drawing Board

Before we can begin to draw up the blueprints for debt-free national economies, we must journey back in time and rediscover the causes that led to the invention of money in the first place. We need to remind ourselves that "money," as such, was never a true preamble to anything. It was incidental to, and came after, the only true preamble found in the entire history of economics: *exchange.*

Money was never an immutable or indispensable artifact of history. God did not create money—man did. And man created it to serve as a medium of exchange. It was to have been a means to an end, never an end in itself.

Another Look at Barter

Let us remind ourselves that at one time "barter" was a viable system of exchange. It was decentralized. It was self-tending and self-limiting. No "inflation" was possible. There was no money to hoard or to speculate with. No one could incur an undeserved loss due to "currency depreciation." No one could obtain an unearned gain due to the "money factor." The whole of the squalid mess associated with junk bonds, derivatives, currency speculation, collateralized debt obligations, mortgage-backed securities, credit default swaps, put options, coffin trades, and Wall Street bet-to-fail shenanigans did not have ground to exist upon. And the "love of money," said to be root of all manner of evil (1 Timothy 6:10), did not yet exist. It's not that barter was the harbinger of utopia on earth, but up to a certain point, barter was a viable and relatively benign system of *exchange*.

Transition from Barter to "Money"

At first the bartering was of the simple sort, face-to-face and one-on-one—a lamb for two pairs of boots, a bushel of corn for a warm cloak, a gallon of milk for a wooden post, etc. But as the centuries went by and organized societies began to emerge, bartering was gradually expanded to involve third and fourth parties until eventually *it became impossible to keep track of who owed what to whom*. That was the point in time when "money" was first introduced as a concept.

Clearly, at a certain point, mankind was obliged to make the transition from barter to money, and thereby endure the sordid history of its falsifications, abuses and misuses, until the day would dawn when a better system could be devised for *keeping track of who owed what to whom*. That day has now arrived.

Global Information Superhighway

With the old order of things fast passing away, it is no mere coincidence that suddenly and only within the last few decades we find at our disposal a revolutionary new system of exchange, made possible by the advent of a global information superhighway that can keep track of who owes what to whom universally and in real time.

The seismic shift is already afoot. Millennial economics is not only within the reach of mankind, it is already facilitating the exchanges of billions of dollars of goods and services throughout the world daily. The whole world is now beginning to exchange goods and services directly, without use of "money," letting the limitations of distance and time between trading partners be taken up by the efficient, fast, accurate, and inexhaustible inventions of the information age.

Visionary Pioneers of the Information Age

What began with the spadework of Charles Babbage and Alan Turing (early computer pioneers) and was later improved by the legacies of Bill Gates and Paul Allen (cofounders of Microsoft); Steve Jobs and Steve Wozniak (cofounders of Apple); Tim Berners-Lee (creator of the Worldwide Web, for which he was knighted by Queen Elizabeth); Andy Grove, Robert Noyce, and Gordon Moore (cofounders of Intel Corporation); Bob Metcalfe and David Boggs (co-inventors of the Ethernet standard for connecting computers); Marc Andreessen (coauthor of Mosaic, the first widely used web browser); Scott McNealy and Bill Joy (cofounders of Sun Microsystems); and many, many other visionary pioneers of the information age now renders millennial economics possible worldwide.

Public Information Utility

If we were to replace the seventeenth-century scaffolding of central banking with a just, fair, and equitable system of exchange, the most holistic, streamlined, and efficient way of doing so would be for Congress to repeal the Federal Reserve Act of 1913, allowing We the People to use the nation's Information Utility as a debt-free medium of exchange.

The Information Utility is already in place, and as of yet no one owns it. To be sure, the central banking institutions that have vested interests in global debt would like to own it and use it to shore up their seventeenth-century scaffolding. But they don't own it. We the People own it.

Nearly all of the components of millennial economics—the communications infrastructures, the software, the hardware, the fiber-optic conduits, the terminals, processors, and databanks—are already in place. Every hour of every day We the People are already using our Public Information Utility to exchange goods and services, pay taxes, fees, etc.

We are already halfway there.

Caution! Caution! Caution!

Admittedly, an optimally streamlined, efficient, and debt-free medium of exchange such as this would be "cashless," and this calls for due caution.

Yes, there is a pitfall here, but the pitfall *can* be avoided, and we must think twice before slaying the goose that lays the golden egg.

Yes, central bankers would like to use a "cashless" system to shore up their seventeenth-century scaffolding! And no, they are not going to stand by with indifference and allow We the People to use our own Public Information Utility to upset their applecart and usher in the era of debt-free national economies. Yes, there is a historic conflict looming.

The historic conflict notwithstanding, the information age is upon us and the global information superhighway is already in place. It now remains for We the People to wake up from the sleep of the dead, come to grips with its emergence, and dispose of its hazards ahead of time, before it can be shanghaied, co-opted, and misused by central bankers.

No, we don't have to waste time explaining that an Information Utility such as this has a great deal of potential, both for good and for bad. But this much is for certain: whether it proves itself a blessing or a curse will in large part depend on *proactive* effort on the part of We the People.

The crossroads are clearly before us. Which will it be? The blessing or the curse? The outcome will depend on what We the People do to protect this new Information Utility from misuse by the powers that be. Will we find the wisdom to apply the lessons of history and render the nation's Information Utility a blessing? Or will we stand by with indifference and allow it to become a curse instead? Rest assured: left unprotected, relegated as a toy into the hands of central bankers, we may yet see the advent of Big Brother and the proverbial *mark of the beast* on earth.

Constitutional Amendment(s)

The First Amendment of the US Constitution reads thus: "Congress shall make no law respecting an establishment of religion, or prohibiting the free exercise thereof; or abridging the freedom of speech, or of the press; or the right of the people peaceably to assemble to petition the government for a redress of grievances."

Who can calculate the sum of mischief that these few words have prevented in the last two centuries? Here are a few words, written on a piece of paper, yet in all the pages of history we would be hard-pressed to find a single blow more severely launched into the ribcage of organized error.

So also, a few words, written into a latter-day constitutional amendment, can serve to protect future generations from untold mischief when it comes to the misuse of the nation's Information Utility and the global information superhighway in general.

Indeed, our elected representatives would do well to earn the gratitude of future generations, just as the Founding Fathers have earned ours, by moving *proactively* to safeguard the nation's Information Utility from misuse.

Don't Make the Same Mistake Again

In passing the Federal Reserve Act of 1913, the US Congress placed its signature on a piece of preferential legislation for which we are now paying a dear price. To avoid a similar error, the nation's Information Utility must be protected by a constitutional amendment, which may read something like the First Amendment itself—an "Economic Bill of Rights," if you will.

Without presuming to dictate the exact wording of such an Amendment, we may nevertheless submit the following suggestion: "Congress shall make no preferential law respecting the use of the nation's Information Utility, or restricting the people's access to it, or applying interest to volumes of trade, or recalling existing moneys, or prohibiting the use of other lawful media of exchange, or hindering the free exchanges of domestic labor and goods."

An Amendment along these lines must be made the law of the land, otherwise We the People will have no ground to complain against the evils that may follow.

In a nutshell: as the nation's Public Information Utility becomes the de facto medium of exchange, Congress must not grant any institution privileged access to it, or a monopoly in the use thereof. The nation's Public Information Utility must at all times be used within the context of a debt-free system of money creation and introduction. And the people must at all times be free to use other lawful media of exchange as well, such as coins, notes, IOUs, etc., which usage embodies one of the basic freedoms of We the People.

Protecting Freedom and Privacy

Congress must protect, *redundantly and comprehensively*, the freedom and privacy of citizens in the use of the nation's Information Utility. Recalling the words of Daniel Webster: "Liberty exists in proportion to wholesome restraint."[22] By the exercise of wholesome restraint, Congress *can* safeguard the liberty, privacy, autonomy, and peace of mind of individuals using the nation's Information Utility as a medium of exchange.

To ensure redundant safety, Congress may also find it necessary to incorporate some of these wholesome restraints into the Constitution. For example, an addendum to the Fourth Amendment might read something like this:

> The right of the people to be secure in the use of the nation's Information Utility shall not be violated and Congress shall make no law enabling invasions of their privacy or property by means of it.
>
> Congress shall make no law requiring RFID chips, skin tattoos, freeze marks or similar abominations to be applied to human beings as a prerequisite to accessing the nation's Information Utility.
>
> Congress shall make no law linking financial transactions (buying and selling) with birth records, employment records, tax records, medical records, insurance records, credit records, driving records, court records, fingerprints, biometrics, voiceprints, palm prints, retinal scans, chromosome imaging, or other marks of identification, in association with use of the nation's Information Utility.

Access Cards

Other than existing social security cards and photo IDs (such as driver's licenses), no national identity card will be issued by government as a

---

[22] Daniel Webster (1782–1852), American Statesman, orator, US senator and secretary of state, during a speech at the Charleston, South Carolina, Bar Dinner, May 10, 1847.

prerequisite to using the nation's Information Utility for trade and commerce. The bank cards that are used to access the Information Utility for buying and selling should be limited in scope to the ATM-type debit and credit cards in use today, which may be issued by the banks of the private sector.

Banks may charge interest on loans (someone using the bank's money to buy something with a *credit* card). However, banks must not be allowed to charge interest on *volumes of trade* in the use of *debit* cards (someone using their own money to buy something, and the bank merely using the Information Utility to electronically transfer the amount from the buyer's account to the seller's account).

No Charging Interest on Volumes of Trade

If, for example, a person goes to a shopping mall and uses a *credit* card to buy an item that costs $1,000, the bank that issued the credit card may charge the buyer interest on the volume of trade ($1,000). Why? Because this person is in effect borrowing the bank's money.

However, if the same person goes to the shopping mall and uses a debit card to buy the item that costs $1,000, the bank may *not* charge either the buyer or the seller interest on the *volume of trade* ($1,000). Why not? Because this person is using his or her own money and all the bank is doing is using the Information Utility to electronically debit the buyer's account and credit the seller's account. In other words, the charges incurred in the use of debit cards must be *straightforward service charges* similar to those charged by other utilities (phone, gas, electric, etc.).

Why are we belaboring this point? An example will show the reason. When you use your debit card to withdraw money from an ATM, the bank that owns the ATM may charge you a *straightforward service charge* of, say, $3.00 for the transaction. It doesn't matter if you are withdrawing $40 or $400, the service charge is still $3.00. That is what we mean by straightforward service charge. (It would make no sense for the bank to charge you interest on ATM withdrawals of your own money.)

"Smart Cards"

It goes without saying that there is enormous potential for both use and misuse in the emergence of government "smart cards." Their proposed applications include everything from streamlined air travel (no passport required), to national and global health-care registries, etc. These devices must likewise be made restrained creatures of law, otherwise We the People will have no ground to complain against the evils that may follow.

Here again, the way to safety lies in transparency, public accountability, disclosure, and Congressional oversight. National security considerations notwithstanding, all government-issued smart cards and Application Specific Integrated Circuit (ASIC) devices, including surveillance contrivances such as cameras, robots and drones, must be periodically declassified and subjected to Congressional oversight. Congress must routinely investigate and publish details relating to *intent, components, and programming.*

Millennial Economics

At this eleventh hour of history, the forces of nature have all but been harnessed to the service of man, not only releasing him from penury and servile dependency but proving false the Malthusian assumption of inveterate scarcity.

Transcendent horizons and limitless objectives are now within the reach of man. Abundance of all good things is no longer a theory. It would be reality, were it not for a crumbling seventeenth-century scaffolding of central banking that is now competing against the labor of man and seeking to deprive him of the dignity of his origins in God.

The advent of the global information superhighway is truly historic, emerging as the holistic antidote to the seventeenth-century scaffolding of central banking. Notwithstanding its pitfalls, some of which we have endeavored to list here, and others which the Congress of the United States will no doubt discover and remedy, mankind, aided by Divine Providence, is destined to employ the global information superhighway as a means of emerging from the oppressive ages of debt.

This is an epochal exodus!

The sudden increases in knowledge and now the arrival of the global information superhighway make that historic transition possible. It could never have been done before. Only recently has technology reached the critical plateau on which millennial economics loomed possible. No generation since the dawn of history could have put such a system into effect!

If the nation's Information Utility is used as a debt-free medium of exchange, and if it is protected from misuse by provisions of righteous law, the streamlined and revolutionary new system of exchange heralded by it will prove an economic blessing surpassing the best we can imagine.

However, if it is not protected from misuse by provisions of righteous law, it will end up being just one more tail that the seventeenth-century scaffolding of central banking will use to wag the dog of human economies in perpetuity. The result? More debt, more poverty, more stagnation, more want, more scarcity, more insecurity, more disorder, more dependency, more natural degradation, more chaos, more tension, more conflict, and more distress, with mass misery with no end in sight.

Should that happen, We the People will have no one to blame but ourselves. This is a call to Revival and Awakening.

Chapter 13

Economic Revolution:
An American Declaration of Independence
from Central Banking

We hold these truths to be self-evident, that all men are created equal, that
they are endowed by their Creator with certain unalienable rights, that
among these are life, liberty and the pursuit of happiness. That to secure
these rights, governments are instituted among men, deriving their just
powers from the consent of the governed.—Declaration of Independence

From slavery in Egypt to freedom in Canaan, from Rome to the Reformation, from serfdom to the Magna Carta, from the Federalist Papers to the Constitution and the Bill of Rights, history catalogs successive eliminations of the institutions that were based on organized error.

To say America has played a key role in the latter-day eliminations of organized error would be an understatement. There is no instance in history where a people so wedded to the archaic, authoritarian, monarchic, oppressive, and defective habits of the Old World were so instantly and effectively set free by the Declaration of Independence in 1776!

In principle, a situation similar to 1776 now presents itself. We the People have it in our power to begin the world over again, with a transition to debt-free national and global economies. The urgency of the occasion; the narrowing of options; the sudden increase of knowledge; the timely emergence of a global information superhighway; and the glorious synchronicity of need, technology, and duty all confirm the imminence of a sea change. The spiritual and the material worlds are about to converge in an enormous value shift—an exodus of biblical proportions.

America's founders did their part to free us politically. We must now do our part to free future generations economically. It now falls upon We the People to pick up where the Founding Fathers left off and complete the historic transformations to which they committed their lives and fortunes with a firm reliance on Divine Providence.

The business before the United States Congress is clear and urgent, and the time to act is now. Tomorrow may be too late. We the People have too much at stake to hesitate. It is our delaying the lawful action that exacerbates the problem. It is our confusion and procrastination that prolongs the ordeal.

By perseverance and right action we have the prospect of a glorious emancipation, not only for ourselves, but also for future generations. By procrastination and submission we have the sad choice of a variety of evils—more debt, more poverty, more want, more conflict, more failure, and more mass misery without mitigation or end.

The three-hundred-year-old debt system of money creation cannot be fixed. It cannot be reformed. It cannot be improved. So transparently has it established itself on earth that it has rendered the whole world blind with respect to its very existence. It is by its very constitution antireform and anti-improvement. It is a debt-creating, debt-compounding system with a built-in "catch 22" that precludes the possibility of reform: all the money and banking courses offered by our institutions of higher learning are built around it! They all teach students of finance how the seventeenth-century scaffolding of central banking creates and introduces new money into circulation *in the form of debt*, the foregone conclusion (the one that escapes all notice) being that this is the *only* way that nations can create their own media of exchange. Well, as has already been shown, this is simply not true. There are better ways of creating/introducing medias of exchange.

When a thing is originally wrong, amendments do not make it right. On the contrary, they may do as much mischief one way as good the other. It is no use trying to "amend" the seventeenth-century scaffolding of central banking. You can't fix something that is broken on the basis of the same set of assumptions that broke it in the first place—you will bounce off the same walls and end up right back where you started.

It is time for a sea change.

So where do we start?

In great endeavors of every kind, the first steps are often the most difficult. Fortunately for us, those first steps were taken by our Founding Fathers. We're already halfway there! And as for the remaining half, if there be any cause for hesitation, it is because no plan has yet been laid down. Therefore, as an opening into this historical undertaking, and as a prelude to formulating a detailed plan, we must pause to take stock and inventory of the political tools that America's founders placed at our disposal.

"Of the People, by the People, and for the People"

The Declaration of Independence affirmed that governments are established to protect the God-given rights of man, and derive their just powers *from the consent of the governed*. Meaning there is no lawful-arbitrary authority in America. Meaning here in America all lawful governmental authority has to be delegated by We the People.

The Constitution and the Bill of Rights were drawn up to indemnify future generations from the encroachments of arbitrary authority. When Congress makes a law, it cannot do so arbitrarily—it must do so within the limits of its constitutional authority delegated to it by We the People.

We would do well to remind ourselves that the theory of the government of the United States is opposed to the unlimited deposit of power in one place. By dividing power among three branches of government, our founders prevented the unlimited deposit of power in one place. By dividing Congress into two houses (a House of Representatives and a Senate), they saw to it that no single group could make laws binding on the whole nation.

Whether the government in question is federal, state, or local, it cannot be a government of one class or group of people—it has to be government of *all* the people. It has to be government *by* the people, because the people elect the officers and representatives to whom they delegate authority. And it has to be government *for* the people, because the government is planned for the good of all the people.

We also need to remind ourselves that any authority delegated by We the People to the government can be taken away from the government by We the People. For example, the authority delegated to the Congress by We the People under the Eighteenth Amendment (prohibiting the manufacture of alcoholic beverages), was taken away by We the People under the Twenty-First Amendment (which repealed the Eighteenth Amendment).

We are a nation of laws. Our laws are made by the Congress of the United States. But the Congress cannot act arbitrarily in the making of them.

How We the People Make Our Laws

Here is a refresher course and quick overview. Generally speaking, bills introduced in the House of Representatives start with the letters "H.R." (for "House Resolution"), followed by a unique bill number. Bills introduced in the Senate begin with the letter "S.," followed by a unique bill number. Money bills cannot be introduced in the Senate—the Constitution gives that important power to the House of Representatives alone. For example, the Federal Reserve Act of 1913 was introduced in the House of Representatives and was designated "H.R. 7837."

Generally, a law begins with a *proposal* to fulfill some public need or to dispose of some public concern. A proposal is called a *bill* only when it is submitted by one of our elected representatives to Congress for consideration and action. A bill can be only submitted to the Congress by a congressman, congresswoman, or senator. A proposal, however, may be submitted by We the People.

Here is a hypothetical and step-by-step exercise: We the People flood the offices of our elected legislators in the House of Representatives with a proposal to repeal the Federal Reserve Act of 1913.

Our proposal becomes a bill when submitted to Congress by one of our elected representatives (a public servant that We the People have elected and pay to act on our behalf).

Then the bill gets referred to the appropriate committee for study. When the committee has finished its study, the bill gets returned to the House to be debated, amended if necessary, voted on, and passed.

After being passed by the House of Representatives, it goes to the appropriate Senate committee for study. Then it gets returned to the Senate to be debated and voted on.

If passed by the Senate, it goes to the president for his signature. Or, if the Senate wants to amend it, it goes to conference for acceptance by members of both the House and the Senate, before being sent to the president.

With the president's signature, the bill become the law that repeals the Federal Reserve Act of 1913.

Many a Slip between the Cup and the Lip

Thousands of bills are introduced in the House and the Senate each year, but many never become laws. Some get pigeonholed (they don't get forwarded to the respective committee for study). But even if they get pigeonholed, *a majority of the members in the House of Representatives may sign a petition to force* the respective committee to study and return the bill to the whole House for debate and a vote. Or, in the Senate, a *majority of senators can elect to take it out of the committee for debate and a vote.*

Even if the president decides to veto the final rendition, *his veto can be overturned by a two-thirds vote of both Houses of Congress.*

This is how laws are made in the United States under the strict guidelines of the Constitution. It's called "American democracy." It can be messy at times, but it works!

The Federal Reserve Act of 1913

The Federal Reserve Act was passed by the Sixty-Third Congress of the United States on December 23, 1913, and signed into law by President Woodrow Wilson on December 24 over the Christmas recess. The original document (H.R. 7837) was twenty-seven pages long, and the following can be found on its first page:

> An act to provide for the establishment of Federal Reserve Banks, to furnish an elastic currency, to afford means of rediscounting commercial paper, to establish a more effective supervision of banking in the United States, and for other purposes.

The following can be found on its last page:

> Sec. 30. The right to amend, alter, or repeal this act is hereby expressly reserved [by the US Congress].

The authority delegated to the Congress by We the People under the Federal Reserve Act of 1913 can be taken away by We the People. The Congress *can* be made to repeal the Federal Reserve Act of 1913 in due process of law. It is not a question of constitutional right, or law, or authority, or power. It is a question of the will, courage, initiative and resolve of We the People.

Our cause is just and the political tools the founders have placed at our disposal are up to the task. Anytime we choose, We the People can use the virtues of the American political system to bring about an economic sea change *in due process of constitutional law.*

Granted, central bankers will employ an army of lawyers, domestic and international influence peddlers, lobbyists, so-called "experts" and media pundits to resist, divert, sidetrack, stonewall, and pigeonhole our efforts at every turn. But We the People will persevere. And God willing, we will prevail.

The Commerce Clause of the Constitution

Pursuant to a successful repeal of the Federal Reserve Act of 1913, the very next order of business (just as important as the repeal itself), will be for Congress to move with speed and efficacy to enact the upright laws that initiate, expedite, and safeguard the historic sea change.

The Constitution gives the Congress specific powers to do just that. Article 1, Section 8, Paragraph 3 of the Constitution, for example, empowers the Congress, "To regulate commerce with foreign nations, and among the several states, and with the Indian tribes."

Realizing that with the passage of time new forms of commerce would emerge needing to be regulated by the United States Congress, America's founders chose not to define or limit the meaning of "commerce." As a result of their foresight it has been possible, for example, to hold that telephone, telegraph, radio, television, and other media are engaged in interstate commerce, and hence the Congress has a power to enact laws regulating their activities in the interest of We the People.

Since the nation's Information Utility is now being used for commerce across state boundaries, the Congress has the authority and obligation to enact laws that would protect and regulate it under Article 1, Section 8, Paragraph 3 of the Constitution. (See chapter 12 for a proposed framework of such legislation.)

Recapping Our Providential Mandate

By picking up where America's Founders left off, We the People are about to write a new chapter in the archives of liberty using the pen and ink of the Constitution and the Bill of Rights. The writing of this new chapter will involve three distinct steps, in principle similar to those that founded the nation. To reiterate:

1) Open a rigorous debate in the bicameral chambers of the US Congress, investigating:
    (i) The purpose and role of "money" in human affairs.
    (ii) The deleterious effect of the seventeenth-century scaffolding of central banking on said purpose and role.
    (iii) Alternate, debt-free methods of money creation, with a view toward promoting economic durability, avoiding inflation, and ensuring public accountability.
2) A unanimous Declaration of Independence by all fifty States of the Union from the now-obsolete providences of central banking institutions.
3) The inauguration of a debt-free system of money creation within the framework of an economic Bill of Rights.

Given the magnitude of the changes proposed and the watershed moment in world history, We the People may, with careful deliberation and with due caution, elect to call together a constitutional convention to dignify the proceedings and to seal the benefits thereof for future generations.

An American Declaration of Economic Independence from Central Banking

In calling for a Declaration of Economic Independence from Central Banking, We the People are not biased by motives of revenge, malice, or resentment toward the central bankers themselves. On the contrary, we pray for them, asking God to make the scales fall from their eyes so they can see the harm they are doing to people, nations, and the planet itself. God forbid that in this historic undertaking we should be found proceeding according to the instincts of the mob that the earth vomits forth at times like this, shaking wicked fists in the air, rattling sabers, crying "conspiracy," and looking for a scapegoat to blame its own failures on.

In this historic undertaking, We the People are resolved to proceed in an orderly fashion and *in due process of law*, doing so because we are honestly, positively, logically, holistically, justifiably, and conscientiously persuaded that an American Declaration of Independence from central banking is in the best interest of mankind.

As it was in 1776 when a people so wedded to the errors of the Old World were so instantly and effectively set free by a political Declaration of Independence, so let it be said by future historians that a people so wedded to the errors of the seventeenth-century scaffolding of central banking were so instantly and effectively set free by an economic Declaration of Independence in our time.

Europe is wedded to the same crumbling seventeenth-century scaffolding and is now groaning in debt: Greece is tottering. So is Italy. So is Spain. So is Portugal. So are most of the nations of the world! The whole earth is groaning under the oppressive yoke of debt, crying out to God for deliverance. Let America rise to the occasion. Let America fulfill her God-given destiny. Let America take the initiative. Let America lead the way to a debt-free world inhabited by free, happy, healthy, prosperous people. Let America do it for the glory of God and the comfort of man's distress.

As goes America, so goes the world. It will indeed take an *American* Declaration of Economic Independence to begin disentangling the world from the ubiquitous tentacles of central banking. It will take an *American* breakthrough to redirect the feet of the world toward sustainable peace and prosperity.

Compromise will not fix the problem, it will only prolong it. Procrastination will leave monstrous debts to our children and with it the sword, famine, and pestilence. Patchwork will mean shrinking back at a pivotal moment in world history when, a little more, a little farther, would have severed the ties, broken the chains, and disenthralled our nation and the world economically.

It is not every nation that can boast of so fair and blessed an origin as the United States. Now more than ever the inspired words of Christ must guide our path: "For unto whomsoever much is given, of him shall be much required. And to whom men have committed much, of him they will ask more" (Luke 12:48).

We the People have been given a providential mandate to make the world a happy place again. We have been given a unique opportunity to exhibit in the theater of history the very nature of economic liberty. To have, as it were, the destiny of the world and the lives and fortunes of billions entrusted to our care is a historic responsibility that we dare not take lightly. It is a providential duty and mandate that we must receive gratefully, shoulder courageously, bear with dignity, and discharge faithfully.

An American Declaration of Economic Independence from Central Banking will enable us to take the first and most important step toward fulfilling our providential mandate and destiny. It will provide opportunities for healing, renewal, restoration and inspiration. It will enable us to extend to an oppressed and debt-ridden world the hand of help and recovery which shall bury in forgetfulness every former conflict and bitterness.

It will stand for a new birth of freedom, for America first, and for the whole world by rapid extension. Its date will be set aside by the congregations of humanity and congress of nations to mark the calendar of the world with an auspicious *jubilee*, a historic renewal, a joyous holiday, and a happy festival, observed throughout the earth by celebrations, convocations, fanfare, fireworks, the ringing of church bells, and the blowing of trumpets.

Index

D

E

F

G

H

www.ingramcontent.com/pod-product-compliance
Lightning Source LLC
Chambersburg PA
CBHW032020170526
45157CB00002B/787